Computer-Security Technology

Computer-Security Technology

James Arlin Cooper
Sandia National Laboratories

LexingtonBooks
D.C. Heath and Company
Lexington, Massachusetts
Toronto

Library of Congress Cataloging in Publication Data

Cooper, James Arlin.
  Computer-security technology.

  Bibliography: p.
  Includes index.
  1. Computers—Access control. 2. Electronic data processing depart-
ments—Security measures. I. Title.
QA76.9.A25C67   1984   001.64'4   82–49206
ISBN 0–669–06436–X

Copyright © 1984 by D.C. Heath and Company

Fourth printing, February 1986

Published simultaneously in Canada

Printed in the United States of America on acid-free paper

International Standard Book Number: 0–669–06436–X

Library of Congress Catalog Card Number: 82–49206

Contents

Figures and Tables

Figures

Tables

Preface

Computers are omnipresent in our daily lives and are becoming more pervasive every day. The word *computer* once was limited to mean a room full of equipment housed in a centralized location and manned by operational personnel. Certainly these types of computing centers remain an important part of computing. However, the discipline is no longer so straightforward. Minicomputers, superminis, microcomputers, shared-resource computing, and distributed computing dominate computer usage in terms of numbers of users, numbers of computers, and hours of computation.

Mainframe computers in computing centers still exist, just as they did in the early days of computing, over thirty years ago. However, disk drives, automatic tape handlers, laser printers, graphics output media, technical control centers, and similar innnovations are common. Few key punches and card readers are used. As the sheer physical size of computers has dramatically decreased, throughput has risen equally dramatically.

Minicomputers have rapidly spread throughout business and industry. Many small businesses and technical organizations that formerly relied on a central computing site now have their own minicomputers. Microcomputers and personal computers are the next step in the evolution. Most micros can provide such an intimate level of service that they are located on a person's desk at the office, workstation, or in the home.

Shared-resource computing is best exemplified by the pervasive terminals, along with modems and acoustic couplers. These developments allow people to operate on a central computer from their offices, homes, hotel rooms, and any other location that can be connected from a remote portable terminal to the computer through direct wiring or through telephone. Time-sharing software within the central computer allows apparently simultaneous activity by a large number of users. Each transaction by a user requires a relatively small share of the computer. Many transactions can be carried out sequentially without any significant impression to any of the users that the computer is being shared.

Distributed computing gives users the ability of using more than one computer to perform a task. If a particular resource is out of service, overloaded, or otherwise inappropriate, the user may select or request an alternative. If a job is best done with processing (sequential or parallel) on more than one computer, this may be possible.

Several computer functions can be performed from one terminal. A small computer is commonly used in preparation, editing, and preprocessing before production activity on a large computer, all from the same terminal. Files can be shipped back and forth between computers, output can be obtained from various computers, and communication can take place between users of a computer or interconnected system of computers.

Shared-resource computing, distributed computing, and multiple computer access from a common terminal are developments that have opened up new and complex requirements for interconnection (see figure P-1). At one time, a few hardwired connections were made to join components, all within a computer center, but now it is not uncommon to find hundreds of terminals connected to computers through various forms of switching and controlling devices such as statistical multiplexers and port contenders. The interconnection is made through various forms of conducting media, such as twisted pairs, coaxial lines, fiber-optic cables, and telephone lines. The communication link sometimes involves microwaves and may even occur via satellite transponder. Technical control centers provide a centralized location for communication equipment and are used for automatic switching and control and remote diagnostics.

Nor is the changing environment limited to pure computing. The way we handle information in general is changing significantly. One of the central contributors is the microprocessor. In the early 1970s, some important developments began taking place. A decade of experience with integrated circuits allowed developers to condense large numbers of components into small areas. With the ability to fabricate thousands of electronic components on a single semiconductor substrate or chip, it became possible to fabricate the basic logic for a computer in a device comparable in size to a fingernail. This microprocessor device quickly became an important part of logic design. In concert with memory devices, an incredible array of products followed that would not otherwise have been possible such as pocket calculators, digital watches, video games, and intelligent terminals.

This programmable logic circuit has put significant computing power in the hands of a large number of people because of its low cost and ease of manufacture. This and similar hardware advances have given users capabilities that would have been beyond their wildest dreams a few years ago. We, as a society, are privileged to be using these developments. It is truly astounding that such great strides are being made in computational capability, speed, size, and power consumption while the cost of the technology is steadily decreasing in an inflating economy.

During the 1970s, many of us concluded that a revolution was taking place—a revolution in our ability to build small, low-cost intelligence into products. A decade later, hindsight reveals that we were at least slightly off the mark. The importance of the revolution that is taking place appears to be in the way we handle information. This revolution is generating powerful new ways for us to handle the information that we deal with in our daily lives. The data we process includes office information (word processing,

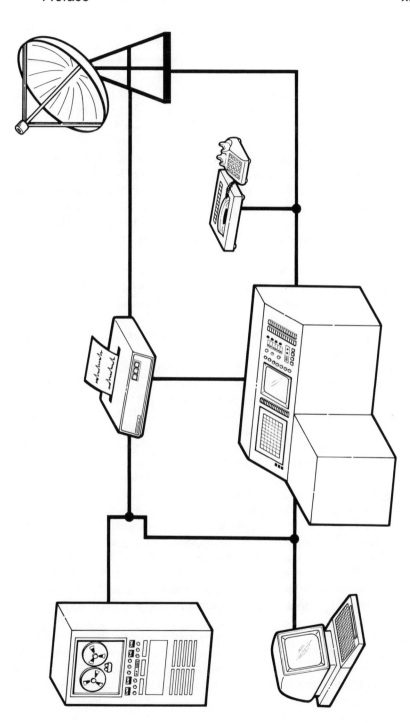

Figure P–1. Computer Interconnnections

telephone calls, memos, information storage and retrieval, calendar data, meetings scheduling, graphics presentation), mailed information (letters, advertisements, news, data), and computer-processed information. Because microprocessors and similar information-processing devices can be built on inexpensive chips, we are moving toward a world were the mails will not be overloaded, where our files will not be bulging, where "telephone tag" is minimized, and where scheduling and information retrieval are rapid and reliable.

This transition has many implications (some painful) for all of us. It may not be too many years before a person who refuses to use computer terminals, office workstations, and other information-processing tools will not be accepted in the office force. Society must also adjust to a certain amount of philosophical change. Bills and records are becoming so highly computerized that it is difficult to communicate about errors, changes, and misunderstandings. Increasingly, our complaints are met with the reply: "The computer did it. It will be straightened out next month." We must also adjust to having our children learn more about computers in elementary school than most of us learned in a lifetime of schooling. It will become as common for a worker to take a terminal home to do after-hours work as a briefcase. We are deluged with new jargon: software, chips, modems, user-friendly, and many other terms.

Computer-security professionals see still deeper implications. We once dealt almost exclusively with central-site security. When the main computer activity was in a central location, it was easy to physically keep unauthorized people away from the computing area. Administrative controls allowed for the powerful "separation of duties" concept, where the people operating the computers were not the ones writing the software routines on which they were operating. There were checks and balances, and it was relatively easy to decide how to implement a computer-security program.

Now a distributed computing environment dominates. If there is a central site at all, it may well be unmanned. The weight of activity, both operationally and in data processing, is shifting to distributed locations where the majority of the human interaction may be done on standalone computers or intelligent terminals. Along with this movement of function, we must also shift our perspective on computer security. We need to view the world as one in which individuals have unprecedented control, for good or for bad. Our security programs must be tailored to meet the new computing environment.

Crucial to meeting these challenges is understanding the technological foundations on which the environment is built. It is dangerous to implement measures for which all the implications are not fully appreciated. Too many security leaks have occurred because someone did something that was unexpected by those who designed or installed the security safeguards. Sometimes the unexpected acts have been the result of shrewd analysis; more often they have been the result of accidental or exploratory sequences of events. In either case, the best chance of having a comprehensive security program results if those handling the security features thoroughly understand the technical aspects of the system they are protecting. It is equally as important to understand the technical aspects of the protective systems themselves.

Computer-security specialists must formulate a comprehensive program based on expert technological knowledge. Otherwise, opportunistic people will seek the chance to do wrong. Violators range from those who see a potential to steal large amounts of money with relatively low risk of apprehension to those who would like to obtain protected information without proper authorization. "Petty theft" is a new problem—employees misusing computer resources by playing personal games or doing personal business activities on a company computer.

Fortunately, although new technology has in many ways made the computer criminal's job easier, it has also provided effective new tools for combatting computer abuse. Computer-security programs can take advantage of technological measures in addition to procedural controls and personal vigilance. Anyone interested in computer security should be interested in understanding this technology.

The other side of the issue is that a book of this sort may also provide valuable information to a computer criminal. Although literature on any subject carries the risk of misapplication, I strongly feel that the balance of value rests clearly in favor of those trying to enhance computer security, for several major reasons:

1. No secrets are revealed in this book. All the problems and techniques discussed are available in published literature.
2. A computer-security administrator who can assemble a program from a wide selection of technologies and techniques is more likely to make intelligent decisions in implementing a comprehensive program than one who is unaware of all of the choices. A comprehensive security program is effective, even if all of its constitutents are known. For example, the knowledge that passwords are encrypted, even if the encryption algorithm is known, discourages attempts to probe database areas for passwords. The type of protection provided by keeping encryption keys secret is more crucial than technical knowledge about the encryption technique used.
3. There is a large class of safeguards for which crucial details of administration at a particular site are not revealed.
4. Systems that are well understood by both the protectors and the attackers have generally proved to be the least vulnerable.

5. Knowledge of techniques used is often actually a deterrent. This situation is somewhat analogous to Internal Revenue Service audit procedures. The fact that audit checks are made is a deterrent to dishonest claims.

This book is an endeavor to present enough information about the technology so that the necessary understanding is provided or the course to be pursued in obtaining complete information is indicated. I hope that readers will derive an overall technical acquaintance with computer-security technology.

The book is organized into three general parts. Chapters 2 and 3 survey the constituents that are used in contemporary computing. This background establishes the basis from which safeguards can be examined. Chapters 4, 5, and 6 portray technology-based protective measures.

Chapter 7 covers a subject that usually receives too little attention by computer-security practitioners. In the press to install sufficient protective measures, we often neglect seeking a report card. Some form of feedback is valuable in determining what measures are working and how well.

The depth to which technology should be pursued in a book of this nature is not easily determined. Technology will be considered to comprise hardware devices, software routines and procedures that have required some degree of unusual development. Some of the subjects included are highly technical and a complete description would be beyond the scope of the book. Others are little more than routine. I have mentioned many of the latter with generally brief descriptions.

In addition to a computer-security reference, I intend that the book be usable as a textbook for a survey course in computer security at the senior or graduate level.

Appendix A is a partial alphabetical list of suppliers of computer-security technology with addresses and phone numbers. Appendix B categorizes vendors by specialty. An extensive glossary of computer and computer-security terms is also included.

I am grateful to a number of persons who contributed their knowledge, time, and energy to this book. Blaine Burnham, Pat Chisholm, Charlie Clendenin, Vern Duke, Mike Eaton, Tom Edrington, Skip Egdorf, Jerry Esch, Russ Hall, Al Iacoletti, Bill Jackson, Craig Jones, Paul Lemke, Mike Lindhorst, Russ Maxwell, Pat Manke, Kelly Montoya, Susan Navarro, Bob Parker, Lyndon Pierson, Don Pitts, Don Schroeder, Tom Schultheis, Gus Simmons, and Bob Trudo read parts of the manuscript and made excellent suggestions. These and other colleagues also provided stimulating exchanges of ideas during office visits, conferences, and correspondence exchanges. In the end, of course, we didn't all agree on my final manuscript. However, their reviews substantially improved what I would otherwise have written.

The manuscript was typed by my wife, Dana. She not only endured this tedious process, but also provided a home environment conducive to (and probably necessary for) the production of a book.

Accuracy was an important objective for all of us, but the final responsibility for the contents is mine. If any errors remain, they are inadvertent. No offense, slighting or misrepresentation of any company, situation or viewpoint is intended.

1 Introduction

Just after 6 p.m. a tall man in a gray business suit walks briskly down the street toward the Franchise Imperial Bank. He is carrying a briefcase. Inside the bank building, most of the employees have gone home. However, there is a hum of activity in the computer room. Many of the bank's most important transactions take place during these evening hours. The in-house balances have already been reconciled, the transactions made in person and by mail have been totaled, and interest, charges, credits and accounts payable have been computed. It has been a full day for the bank's computer. It has served as an accounting information source, a calculating tool, and a word processor. In addition to routine bookkeeping, it has generated over 100 form letters, 1,500 bank statements, and 2 issues of advertising copy.

But this time of evening is special. Money must be moved electronically between banks. Each bank honors thousands of checks from other banks every day. Many of these transactions take place electronically. In addition, data on interbank loans, reference data, and routine communications must be processed. Electronic transmission has the advantage of high speed, low cost, and accurate accounting. All that is required is a computer and a communication link.

Franchise Imperial Bank uses its computer for just such transactions at night because computers are too expensive to sit idle for more than a short time. Its computer room is active 24 hours a day.

The man in the gray business suit times his approach to the front door just as a bank employee leaves and catches the door before it snaps securely shut in a locked position. He strides briskly down the hall, pleased with his good fortune. No one questions an official-looking person who seems to be doing just what he has a right to do. However, if he had not entered the bank just as an employee left, he could have entered during business hours and hidden in the rest room; he could have bribed that computer operator who always frequented the corner bar, drinking too much and talking too much; he could have bypassed the lock with a skillful pry of his screwdriver.

But now is the time for action. He locates the telephone junction box. Like so many banks, Franchise Imperial uses ordinary telephone lines to transmit all of its precious financial data—and money. The box is not locked, so the man opens it. Inside is a maze of wires, but his practiced eyes

*quickly scan the labels. "E4 intercom," "Line 7," "Computer Line"—
Computer Line!*

*The man opens his briefcase. It contains no papers, no books, no
ledgers, but rather two inductive line pickups, a datascope, a microcomputer, and some simple tools. The easy availability of microcomputers
makes his job so much easier! His briefcase holds as much capability in
terms of computational complexity as the first mainframe computers. But
his microcomputer runs on a battery and is thousands of times cheaper and
more reliable than those early computers.*

*The man has done his homework well. He knows that the transactions
are checked for accuracy with a cyclic redundancy check. CRC checking has
been developed mainly to combat the kind of random errors that can occur
because of "noise" on the lines from lightning, power surges, electromagnetic interference, and other environmental hazards.*

*The theory is simple. In addition to the information content of a
message (invariably represented by a sequence of binary digits or "bits"), a
relatively small number of "check" bits are added according to a mathe-
matically based relationship that has been well established in the study of
error-correcting codes. The check bits allow a reasonably certain (better
than 99.99 percent, in the case of the Franchise Imperial Bank code) check
on the integrity of the transaction. But not 100 percent! And therein lies the
strategy of the man in the gray business suit. He knows from his conversations with bank employees that they have relaxed and come to rely on the
code as an authenticity and accuracy check, for which it was never intended.*

*Clipping an inductive probe onto the computer line, he switches on the
miniature datascope. He first verifies the computer data, a simple step. A
stream of computer bits dance across the screen. With a quick flip of a
switch the microcomputer hums into action, passively monitoring data.
Next, he places an output probe on the line. With keyboard entry, the microcomputer swings into action, computing check bits that fit the code. But
what is the code? That is the beautiful part. The code isn't important. In
fact there are thousands of codes that would give the same check digits.
Only one of them is being used by the bank's computer, but there were over
50 million possible bit patterns that could occur. Because of this magnitude,
the code designers understand that an error is extremely unlikely to result in
a pattern with the same check bits as the intended transmission. That is the
contribution of error-correcting codes—a high degree of protection with
only a few check bits.*

*A low buzz signals to the man that an appropriate code with the same
check bits has been discovered. A quick snip of the wire, and the microcomputer will be in control, delivering bit sequences that consistently fit the pattern but are in fact random transactions. Funds will be electronically
diverted in enormous amounts. Because the check bits fit, there will be no*

indication of malfunction. By the time the auditors discover the discrepancy, the bank accounts will be in a shambles. The events leading up to the scramble may never be unraveled and the auditors will have a major task determining whether any funds have been stolen.

The man smiles. He is just playing a game—beating a system to prove he can do it. However, he is the head of a company that insures banks and other institutions against losses and disruptions resulting from computer crime. He has been in contact several times with the Franchise Imperial Bank. He will be in contact with them again in about a month, when the impact of his computer-created funds diversion has been fully appreciated.

Now, he is ready. A clean cut, a few minutes of computer-generated havoc, a simple repair, and he will be done. Equipment back in the briefcase, a brisk official-looking exit, and he can relax. He cuts the wire. Suddenly the air is filled with a piercing wail of an alarm. He hears curt voices and running footsteps. His heart beats fiercely. He knows something has gone wrong. But what? He used the most advanced technology possible. He thought through every aspect of his plan. He knew it would succeed!

The man in this narrative lost a battle fought with computer-security technology. The bank had recently installed an encryption scheme that prevented data analysis. The encrypted data was checked for authentication. When the authentication check failed, a system alarm was triggered.

This incident is fictional. Obviously, most banks have physical and electrical protection far superior to Imperial's. However, it illustrates an ongoing struggle between those who would operate outside the law, without respect for the rights of others, and those who are computer-security professionals. Their job is to protect computers against misuse and vandalism; to safeguard computer data from unauthorized disclosure or manipulation; and to recommend cost-effective modes of protection to businesses. Their goal is to minimize the possibility of computer crime and misuse without interfering with everyday business.

Computer security has received notable attention in recent years for many reasons. Public and professional interest has been stimulated by reports of dramatic computer crimes involving huge sums of money. Although some very serious incidents have occurred, the extent to which computers contributed is often exaggerated. Over $400 billion is transferred daily over U.S. electronic financial networks. Because such large transactions are routinely being made electronically with computer driven devices, a concern for security is certainly justified.

In addition, a relatively unfamiliar technology is pervading our lives. The less we, as a society, understand it, the more we fear what it might possibly do to harm us. While we often tend to overreact to unfamiliar threats, it is healthy that we do not take them too lightly. Third, the U.S. government has enacted some significant computer-security legislation. Government agencies and their contractors have been ordered to formulate strong computer-security programs and to review their effectiveness periodically. The fourth reason for the interest in computer security should be the most important of all: computer security is simply good business practice.

Every computer-security measure should be cost-effective. Very few if any of these measures are cost-free. If the value to the company or business of the protective measure does not justify its cost, the measure shouldn't be taken.

What does "computer security" mean? Before trying to put the information in this book to use, one should understand the ground rules. For many people, computer security immediately brings to mind protection against computer-driven transfers of funds to unauthorized sources. However, I take the broader view that computer security should be defined to represent protection of information and protection of physical and personnel assets. That is, computer security comprises both information security and physical-assets security.

Each area can be further subdivided. Information security can mean protection against unauthorized disclosure, manipulation, destruction, or alteration. Unauthorized disclosure refers to the receipt of protected information, such as classified information, information subject to the Privacy Act of 1974, or proprietary information. Unauthorized manipulation refers to changing some attribute of the data, such as file ownership, data destination, or classification. Data destruction means erasure. Information can be destroyed, for example, by overwriting, degaussing, or by removing power from a volatile memory. Data alteration means introducing numerical or character changes—for example, changing financial amounts, changing measured values, or changing system control parameters. In summary, information security should provide at least the following protections:

Protection against unauthorized disclosure

Protection against unauthorized movements

Protection against unauthorized purging

Protection against data changes

Physical-assets security refers to theft, destruction, or misuse of computer-system property (including computers, peripherals, and data-storage media). Theft is usually motivated by the value of the property stolen, but can be strictly malicious. Destruction can be accidental (from earthquake, fire, or flood) or intentional (vandalism or terrorism).

Misuse includes activities that are not considered proper by the management responsible for the computer. Examples might include conducting personal computations or business, or playing games for personal entertainment.

In summary, physical-assets security protects against theft, destruction, and misuse.

In addition, a comprehensive program protects personnel assets—those people associated with computers. Such protection has the dual purpose of ensuring personal safety as well as the availability of those with the operational skills to make computing a company asset.

It is also appropriate to define technology, at least in the the context of this book. A typical dictionary definition is "applying science to achieve a practical purpose." In this book, technology means procedural techniques, hardware devices, and software routines that are based on analytical designs or developments. Although a broad definition, it covers the breadth of the subject matter included here.

It is also necessary to specify what a computer is. This definition determines the realm of devices over which computer security should be exercised. This determination is not easily made. For one thing, there is a large spectrum of devices that do some form of computing. Basic calculators and controllers that are not easily user-programmable are generally not included in a computer-security program. Many computing devices may or may not be of interest, depending on the view of those responsible. In this book, our interest will encompass large computers, medium (midi- and mini-computers), and microcomputers, as well as such office-automation devices as word processors, electronic mail, and voice processing devices.

2 Hardware Constituents

As a prelude to describing protective measures, this chapter addresses the hardware constituents that must be protected. Just as computer-security protective measures are heavily based on current technology, so are computer systems and peripheral components. The following overview of these constituents provides a foundation for describing computer-security technology. Before examining protection, it is important to consider what it is that must be protected, and to consider the resultant security implications. Hardware is the first important category. Hardware constituents are tangible pieces of equipment associated with data-processing, information-processing, or computing activities. Hardware comprises the physical entities that must be protected in a computer-security program.

Hardware falls generally into three categories: computing and data-processing equipment, peripheral components, and communication links.

Computing and Data-Processing Equipment

Mainframe Computers

Mainframe computers are the large backbone computers around which centralized computing has been built. After an intriguing sequence of developments, general-purpose computers for commercial applications began to appear in the 1950s. One of the first mainframes was the UNIVAC I, developed by Remington Rand. The public took special notice of the computer when the 1952 election projections were relayed nationwide by Walter Cronkite.

Contemporary computing centers containing mainframe computers have many similarities to their counterparts of thirty years ago. There are still operators, control consoles, memory devices, and other peripheral equipment. However, during the last thirty years mainframe computers have utilized developing technology to beome faster, smaller, computationally more powerful, less power-consuming, and easier to program and operate. From a security viewpoint, the increased complexity and dispersal of users presents new challenges.

7

Superminicomputers

Minicomputers have been in general use for nearly twenty years. Minicomputers were developed as special-applications devices and were later enhanced to serve as general-purpose computers. A powerful new class of minicomputer appeared on the marketplace a few years ago. These machines are variously called midicomputers, superminicomputers, or simply superminis. As might be expected, these computers are about midway between minicomputers and mainframe computers in performance, cost, size, and general capabilities. Generally, they include multiple-user interactive processing, queuing, and word lengths of 32 bits or more.

Minicomputers

Minicomputers are small computers that are typically of suitable size for placement on desks, tables, or in equipment racks. They are also distinguished from their larger cousins by generally smaller word lengths, more restricted computational capabilities, smaller memories, and less (if any) capacity for handling more than one user at a time.

Microcomputers

Defining the various types of computers is not as straightforward a task as might be implied by the previous descriptions. There is a blur of capabilities, making it unclear where to draw a definitive line. Quite often, the most distinguishing characteristic is the name chosen by the manufacturer. Unclear as the situation may be for the types of computers described previously, it is even less clear for distinguishing microcomputers from minicomputers. Microcomputers are intended for personal use, either in the home (personal computers) or at work (business computers). They are generally not as well supported as minicomputers in terms of software, peripherals, servicing, and security features.

Most microcomputers are built around a single microprocessor, but some use multiple microprocessors. However, microprocessors can conceivably be used in one form or another in any size computer. Larger computers use microprocessors for peripheral functions as opposed to their central role in microcomputers (and some minicomputers).

Controllers

It is common to use a device that has computational capability for tasks other than general-purpose computing or data processing. One of the most

common uses is as a dedicated controller—that is, only a restricted operation can be performed, with insertion of control parameters rather than
general programs. Examples include control of manufacturing processes,
control of testing operations, flow control (such as traffic signals), control
of automobile functions (such as cruise control, carburetor mixture), control of calculations (hand calculators), and control of time and calendar
indicators (digital watches). Early minicomputers were used as controllers.

A controller may or may not have computer-security implications
according to whether sufficient harm can occur due to unsecure operation.
For example, control of a critical process (mixing of explosives or centrifuge
speed control) may warrant integrity measures. However, control of a
digital watch creates no security problems. Generally, the computer-security
interest in computing aspects of controllers decreases with computational
capabilities and users' ability to gain access for user-controlled processing.
For example, a mainframe computer that both controls a process and is also
available for user programming would typically be scrutinized; a noncritical
controller with its program imbedded in ROM would be of no interest.

Word Processors

Word processors are a type of controller used to form, manipulate, and edit
text. Computer-security interest in word processors is based on their storage
of information that may need to be protected. Some word-processor
systems compound this fundamental problem by allowing shared-resource
operation. Just as the differences between minicomputers and microcomputers are blurred, there is no clear way to distinguish intelligent typewriters
from word processors. Additional merging is occurring as microcomputers
gain more word-processing capabilities and word processors gain more
computer attributes.

Distributed Systems

Distributed systems implies computing, data-processing, information-
processing, or word-processing systems for which the components are at
multiple physical locations and use interconnections for communication,
data sharing, and distributed processing. The primary computer-security
issues in distributed systems are that communications are generally more
vulnerable to interception, disruption, or alteration; the physical environment is harder to make secure because of its dispersal; and individual users
are generally more in control of the processing than in centralized systems.

Networks. Networks are a type of distributed system that emphasize communication or data transfer and the distances spanned by the network are

relatively great. The actual physical dimensions of networks are highly variable. Local-area networks typically are utilized for communication within a
building or within a local group of buildings; satellite networks can span a
large portion of a hemisphere.

Networks can be structured in a variety of ways, but four topology
models are commonly used to describe the basic strategies. These structures
(or architectures) are shown in figure 2–1.

1. Ring (loop) network (upper left of figure 2–1). This topology is used
   in many local area networks. If the loop is bidirectional, a single break
   in the communication capability will not affect the overall system communication.
2. Star network (upper right of figure 2–1). This form has a central node
   with which all peripheral nodes communicate. In a typical implementation, remote terminals are connected to a host computer.

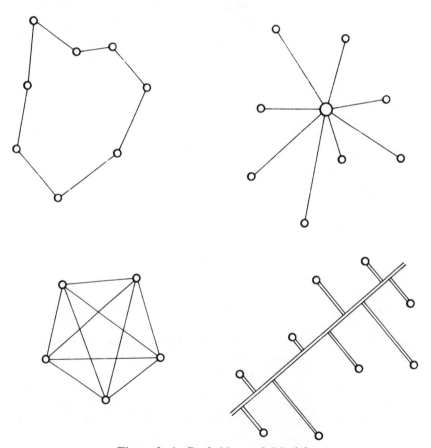

Figure 2– 1. Basic Network Models

3. Bus network (lower right of figure 2-1). This structure has a bus (a conductor system) to which nodes can be connected almost independently of each other. Typical implementations include most microprocessor systems (CPU, ROM, RAM) and many commercial local area networks.
4. Fully interconnected (mesh) network. This structure is conceptually attractive, but demands large numbers of connections.

In practice, these network structures take on many forms, variations, and combinations. The physical dispersal and the data traffic over extensive communication media exacerbate computer security problems.

Office Workstations

Office workstations are computers, terminals, or word processors that are used to assist with such office tasks as text preparation, message transfer, information storage and retrieval, meeting scheduling, tabular compilations of data, and graphic presentations. Some workstations operate as stand-alone units; more commonly, communication and shared-resource processing are involved.

Office workstations present computer security problems because of networking and because individual control prevents separation of duties and other fundamental security measures. Also, commercially furnished security is not generally strong in office automation systems.

Peripheral System Components

Control Consoles

Large computers (such as mainframes and superminis) are ususally controlled by an operator from a console or station. The controlled operations include booting the operating system on-line; initiating program execution; bringing the system down when necessary; prompting operators on system status; and prompting operators with messages on the console display (for example, "No tape loaded on tape unit 3").

Memory Devices

Memory is one of the most important features of a computer system (and one of the most crucial to computer security). Memory devices have evolved through many stages, ranging from electrochemical and mercury delay lines to today's efficient semiconductor memories.

Until the early 1970s, core memories were the dominant computer fast-access memory. Although relatively expensive, their performance and speed were essential to the development of powerful computers. However, integrated circuit technology provided a breakthrough in semiconductor memory capability. As semiconductor memory became competitive with core memory (in terms of cost as well as performance), the use of core memory dropped significantly.

There are two relatively minor computer-security issues in memory devices. First, volatile semiconductor RAM memories are not susceptible to remnant traces of information previously contained and core memories are. In other words, semiconductor memories are easier to purge. In fact, power removal or loss will purge most semiconductor volatile RAM memories; core memory, in contrast, is nonvolatile (data are retained when power is removed or lost). Core memories also require many overwrite cycles to remove memory traces completely. Second, semiconductor memories are more resistant to information tapping while actively storing data (ROMs or RAMs) because the magnetic and electomagnetic fields in the vicinity or semiconductors are much smaller than around cores.

In selecting memory technology, designers have always been faced with a fundamental cost-speed tradeoff. The most inexpensive memories generally allow data retrieval at the slowest access rates. Figure 2–2 shows the general cost-speed performance of various types of memories. Semiconductor and core memories are used where fast access is required. Tape is a much less expensive storage medium, but it is also much slower. It is used mainly for applications with high-volume or slow-access requirements or both. Intermediate to these media (in both cost and speed) are drum and disk memory. Major computer systems use all three types of memory.

When information is not needed immediately, it makes sense to offload data into slower, less expensive memory. Drums and disks are relatively convenient forms. Other less accessible, but less costly forms are magnetic tape, Winchester disks, cassettes, tape cartridges, diskettes (floppy disks), and paper tape. Sometimes automatic tape or cartridge loaders are used. Optical disks are also now in limited use.

Printers/Plotters

Printers and plotters are a crucial interface for computer systems because they typically create the most useful output for users—printed text, numerical data, checks, forms, tables, graphs, plots, and other formats. These devices raise important computer-security issues. For example, the

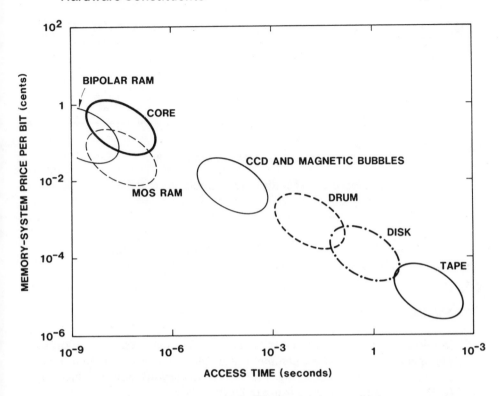

Figure 2-2. Memory Cost/Performance Tradeoff

protection level of the output is often made uniform to prevent possible mixing of protected output with unprotected output. It is also common to control and keep inventory on number of forms used in critical functions (such as paychecks).

Terminals

Terminals are one of the most powerful computing interfaces in use today. Various forms of terminals can be used for interactive computer use, port contender control, and office automation (such tasks as word processing and electronic mail).

Terminals create special computer security problems because of their remote locations and because of their powerful ability to communicate. An example of the latter problem is the "terminal masquerade" attack, where

MULTIPLEXER/DEMULTIPLEXER PAIR

Figure 2-3. Multiplexer/Demultiplexer Pair

special conditions enable a terminal to create a communication with a computer that appears to have originated from another terminal.

Multiplexers

Multiplexers or concentrators are used to consolidate communication by multiple users onto a single communication channel. Three common forms are time-division multiplexing (TDM), frequency-division multiplexing (FDM), or statistical multiplexing (STAT MUX).

Time-division multiplexing essentially assigns each of *n* users one of *n* evenly divided time slots during a multiplex period. Although each user is connected only a fraction ($1/n$) of the time, the period is relatively short so that the multiplexing action is transparent to the users. TDM performance is the high-speed electronic analog to a rotary switch, as shown in figure 2-3. To complete the link, user identification (or demultiplexing) is needed; it requires synchronization of multiplexer and demultiplexer control and is also illustrated in figure 2-3.

Frequency division multiplexers combine data streams onto a common signal. Each user is assigned an input mode that uses a specific frequency for transmission across a channel. The channel links pairs of multiplexers and demultiplexers. Demultiplexing is essentially filtering to isolate the information received at the assigned frequency.

Both time-division multiplexers and frequency-division multiplexers preassign transmission capacity to each user connection, regardless of usage. Statistical multiplexers overcome this shortcoming by adjusting the capacity assignment dynamically in response to processing loads. Their main issues for computer security are that loss of or incorrect synchronization can result in the improper definition of the user source or destination and that crosstalk could potentially put information from or intended for one user on another's line.

Modems

A modem (modulator/demodulator) is a device used to couple interface or peripheral equipment to telephone networks or similar communication links. Modems are available for a large number of frequencies, transmission coding, and protocol techniques, as well as such other capabilities as auto-dialing.

Port contenders. Port contenders are electronic logic switches used to connect a large number n of users to a smaller number m of interactive computer ports. They allow efficient time-sharing utilization of computer ports by a large number of users as shown in figure 2-4.

The contention problem occurs when $n > m$. Port contenters connect the first m users requesting access. Because any additional users cannot be handled by the computer, the port contender denies access until a port becomes free. Many port contenters have the capability to queue surplus users and deliver a message indicating the users's position in the queue. As with multiplexers, inadvertent connection and unintended coupling must be prevented. Some port contenters can be partitioned for additional security protection—that is, classes of user lines can be restricted to corresponding classes of computer ports. For example, classified operation can be partitioned from unclassified operation. In addition, coordinating user disconnects and subsequent user connection with the jobs being processed on the computer poses the danger that a user exchange can be made by the port contender without the corresponding change in the computer. As a result, the second user would be connected to the first user's job stream. Com-

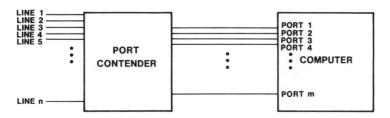

Figure 2-4. Port Contender Concept

munication between the port contender and the computer can prevent this hazard.

Network Gateways

When networks interconnect dissimilar components, or when dissimilar networks are interconnected, communication format (protocol) must be translated. For networks, protocol translation usually is built into a network gateway device, which is usually a relatively small special-purpose computer. Network gateways often handle a diverse array of data traffic. The restriction that all users must not have access to all data is common, in which case gateways are a security concern. However, gateways can use secure or physically controlled hardware and secure software to which users have no access.

Network-Security Controllers

The security for a single computer is relatively straightforward: controls such as user authentication, access control, and privileges are handled within the computer system. However, when two or more computers are interconnected to form a network, the security problem becomes more complex. For example, a user of the computer A system may need access to the computer B system for use of data in a computer B memory file. The user might have authorization built into both systems or computer B might simply accept traffic already authorized by computer A. As more computers (and more security rules) are added, the situation quickly becomes intractable. For this reason a network may have all network-security functions consolidated into a network security-controller, ususally a relatively small special-purpose computer to control the hardware/software and run no user code. Gateway and security-controller functions can be combined in the same computer.

Technical Control Centers

Most modern computer centers are linked to large numbers of remote terminals and computers, typically by port contenders, multiplexers, modems, and switches. Because of the common connection properties and because of the convenience of having a dedicated site for remote diagnostics across a network, technical control centers or communication centers are often used as a central site for the required equipment.

Power and Environment

Quality power is important to system performance, including security. For this reason, power supplies and other environmental controls (for example, air conditioning, smoke and fire detection, water detection, and seismic integrity) must be addressed in a computer-security program.

Communications Links

The dispersal of computing instruments, the desire to communicate between users, the need for each user to utilize multiple computers, the need to share data—all these requirements have dictated the development of communications links. There are many ways to create these links. Unfortunately, information can also be conveyed by unintentional links (such as Tempest) that are described later. This section addresses hardwired links, fiber optics, electromagnetic links, and public-line links all of which offer the potential for passive listening (tapping) as well as signal degradation as speed and propagation distance increase.

Information is communicated in several basic ways, including:

1. Direct transmission. Information is conveyed exactly as processed. For example, logic represented by voltage levels of 0 V. or 5 V. is delivered directly as 0 V./5 V. levels across connecting lines.
2. Amplitude modulation. A carrier conveys information across the communication link. The carrier amplitude is varied to signal the intelligence (see figure 2–5). This method is used in AM radio, television video, and telephone transmission. Digital amplitude modulation is called amplitude-shift keying (ASK).
3. Frequency modulation. A carrier is modulated by varying the frequency to signal the intelligence (see figure 2–6). This method is used in FM radio, TV sound, and most satellite links because of its immunity to random interference or noise. Digital frequency modulation is called frequency-shift keying (FSK).
4. Phase modulation. Intelligence is provided by varying the phase of a carrier. Because frequency and phase are not independent, frequency deviation depends on both the amplitude and frequency or the modulating signal. Digital phase modulation is called phase-shift keying (PSK).
5. Coding. Various forms of coding are used to convert information to digital (usually binary) data. Alphabetic characters, for example, can be coded by standard codes such as the ASCII (American Standard Code for Information Interchange) or EBCDIC (extended binary-

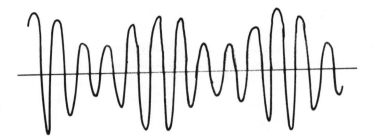

Figure 2–5. Amplitude Modulation

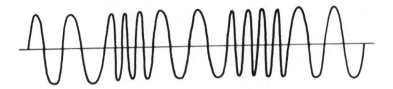

Figure 2–6. Frequency Modulation

coded decimal interchange code). Analog data can also be digitized. This concept, illustrated conceptually in figure 2–7, is to convert an analog representation (like voltage) to the closest binary representation that can be determined. Common coding techniques used for digital data transmission are pulse-code modulation (PCM) and delta (change) modulation (DM).

6. Protocol. Communication protocols include half duplex (information flow in one direction at a time), full duplex (simultaneous bidirectional), synchronous (tied to particular timing constraints), asynchronous (self-timed within a transmitted symbol, which can occur at any time), and isochronous (some features of both synchronous and asynchronous). Other digital codes include the Baudot code (a five-level or five-bit code), the Binary-Coded Decimal (BCD) code, the Manchester code, and the dibit code (phase-dependent on a pair of bits).

Hardwired Connections

Point-to-point wiring without precautions to avoid coupling and reactive effects is impractical, except over very short distances (typically 10 feet or less). Signal quality is important for preserving signal-to-noise ratio;

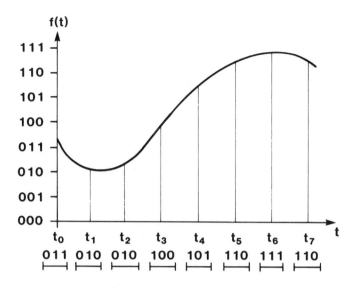

Figure 2-7. Digitizing

and radiated energy can interfere with other electronic equipment or be intercepted.

One approach is to use twisted-pair wiring, which uses the geometrical variation created by the twisting (spiral) pattern to cancel some of the effects that produce capacitance and inductance. This technique is limited to relatively short distances (although not as restricted as point-to-point wiring) and relatively slow signaling speeds without special enhancement measures (on the order of hundreds of feet and tens of kilobits per second). Twisted pairs can be easily shielded (braided or solid). More commonly, they are combined into cables containing multiple pairs with both electrical shielding and physical protection.

A similar technique uses multiconductor flat cable. The proximity of the signal-carrying pairs helps to combat the effects of coupling and interference. Distance limitations are similar to those of twisted pairs. Coaxial cable often is an appropriate choice when twisted pairs cannot be used because of speed or distance requirements. It is usually more expensive than twisted pairs. Coaxial cabling is formed by surrounding one conductor (inner conductor) by another (outer conductor), as shown in figure 2-8. A dielectric separates the conductors. Additional shielding and structural features are often incorporated in the cable.

Routing point-to-point wiring is often complex and requires attention during building design and retrofit, by both planners and designers and computer security personnel. In new buildings, for example, "riser"

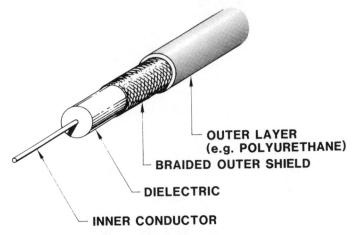

OUTER LAYER
(e.g. POLYURETHANE)
BRAIDED OUTER SHIELD

DIELECTRIC

INNER CONDUCTOR

Figure 2-8. Coaxial Cable

systems are necessary to provide paths between floors and through other similar barriers. Interoffice distribution systems on a single floor require raceways, conduit, or similar channels. Drops from the ceiling or risers from the floor are required to provide connection points for terminals, computers, or other data-processing equipment.

Security considerations frequently dictate that the wiring not be run in common physical channels with telephone or other public lines, and additional physical protection may be required. Esthetic considerations provide further constraints. Retrofitting existing buildings is even more difficult.

Interbuilding wiring requires underground or overhead links. Underground wiring can be made relatively secure, but manholes are necessary for installation and access. All of these wiring systems require junction boxes, in which systems are joined.

A common interconnection technique is to use local-area networks, whereby connection problems are simplified by allowing all users common access to a transmission medium. Security problems arise if the user community does not have uniform needs for or rights to the information.

Fiber Optics

For very high-speed or high-bandwidth applications, fiber-optics is often used because of its performance advantages. Fiber-optic communication is accomplished via light-wave energy (between about 10^{14} and 10^{15} Hz) propagated through tiny fused-glass fibers.

Fiber-optic cables also provide significant security advantages. They

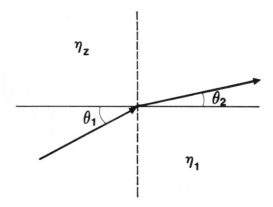

Figure 2-9. Snell's Law Relationship

are harder to tap, and they emanate less (essentially none) than hardwired links, electromagnetic links, or telephone links. Fiber optics are also resistant to RFI (radio-frequency interference) cable coupling, electrical equipment noise, lightning-induced transients, and EMP (electromagnetic pulse). The cables are small, light-weight, and temperature-resistant, in addition to providing reliable transmissions and ground- and common-mode isolation. However, they are relatively complex, high-cost, somewhat fragile systems with relatively difficult break-out, splicing, and termination. In fact, not until the development of new materials with losses on the order of 10 dB/km and less did fiber-optic data communication become practical. Losses are approaching 1 dB/km currently, as removal of water from the glass has improved. Losses have decreased by a factor of about 100 since 1970. The confinement of energy within the fiber-optic material is based on the Snell's Law relationship (figure 2-9)

$$\eta_1 \cos \theta_1 = \eta_2 \cos \theta_2$$

where η_1 represents the index of refraction of the glass and η_2 represents the index of refraction of the surrounding medium (usually a cladding layer with a lower index of refraction than glass.) When $\eta_1 > \eta_2$, as θ_1 becomes small, θ_2 can be forced to 0, after which no transmission can occur through the interface and reflection is complete. This characteristic is the basis for confining light energy inside fiber-optic material. This effect has been known at least since the pioneering work of John Tydall in 1854.

Fiber types in use include single-mode step-index fiber (for monomode transmission of linearly polarized energy), multimode step-index fiber

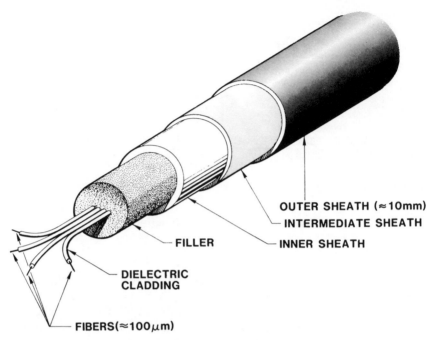

OUTER SHEATH (≈10mm)
INTERMEDIATE SHEATH
FILLER   **INNER SHEATH**
**DIELECTRIC
CLADDING**

FIBERS(≈100μm)

Figure 2–10. Fiber-Optic Cable

(which provides more modes and less bandwidth), and multimode graded-index fiber (the refractive index varies with the distance from the fiber center).

A fiber-optic cable typically contains many cladded fibers and provides a surrounding layer of physical protection (see figure 2–10). Core diameters are on the order of 0.1 mm; cladded diameter is roughly a factor of two higher. Typical energy sources are light-emitting diodes and semiconducting lasers. Typical detectors are PIN diodes and avalanche photodiodes (APDs). Energy attenuation is commonly on the order of 5 dB/km, or less, but laboratory work has demonstrated losses as low as 0.1 dB/km.

Various fiber-optic interface devices are available, including connectors, splicers, optical couplers, amplifiers, modems, and multiplexers. Multiplexing is possible using wavelength-division multiplexing (WDM). Other multiplexing techniques have been developed using dichronic-beam splitters and dielectric-interference filters.

Typical bit error rates (BER) of 10^{-12} and system failure rates (MTBF) of 10^6 hours are achievable in fiber-optic systems. Systems are being installed for local-area networks (distances less than 1 km) and for long-haul transmission. Distances on the order of 100 km without repeaters are feasible with single-mode transmission. Fiber optics will have an important role in future data-transmission links and computer security.

Electromagnetic Links

Some communication links depend on the radiation and propagation of electromagnetic energy through the atmosphere (or similar media such as free space). The characteristics of these communication links depend mainly on radiation-transmission frequency.

Radio Frequency. Historically, the most common communication links have been at radio frequencies (rf), which generally range from megahertz ($\approx 10^6$ Hz) to gigahertz ($\approx 10^9$ Hz). At the lower frequencies, propagation can occur over long distances because of ionospheric scattering and diffraction, but in the VHF (≈ 100 MHz) and UHF (≈ 1 GHz) region, propagation is limited to line of sight. Radio links can be point-to-point or broadcast.

Because radio transmission is used for many applications, channel allocations must be obtained. Regulatory requirements also prevent interference among sources. Other important considerations include the effects of noise (for example, created by lightning) and physical interference (such as buildings or airplanes in the transmission path). Security considerations must include ease of signal interception and interference or jamming.

Very low- (extra low-) frequency radiation (ELF) is used for data communication in special circumstances, such as from land-based transmitters to underwater submarines, because of the deeper penetration depth in water of low-frequency electromagnetic energy. However, data rates are reduced correspondingly to the reduction of frequency.

Tropospheric-scatter (troposcatter) links depend on reflection and scatter of relatively low frequencies (hundreds of kilohertz) from the troposphere. At the upper ends of the radiation spectrum, where data rates can be very high, the major problems are absorptive losses resulting from the atmosphere, clouds, and rain.

Infrared Transmission. Electromagnetic energy in the infrared region (10^{12} to 10^{14} Hz) can be made highly directional, reducing some of the security hazards of rf transmission. The high frequencies enable short high-peak-power pulse transmission. Pulse-rate modulation can be used to reduce atmospheric scintillation effects and background noise. Because of atmospheric absorption, scattering, and other variations, infrared links are limited to approximately 30 km. Typical infrared sources are LEDs, gas lasers, and semiconductor laser diodes. Typical detectors are PIN diodes, APDs, and dynamic crossed-field PMTs.

Satellite Links. The satellite age began with the Soviet and U.S. launches in 1957. Since then, satellite technology has made giant strides. More and more orbiting devices, some incredibly sophisticated, are circling the earth. There are now well over a thousand satellites, many active, some silent. They are used mainly to make measurements and relay communications.

Communications satellites have been used since the early 1960s. The first of these were useful only periodically because they circled the earth at relatively low (hundreds of miles) orbits. In 1945, Arthur C. Clarke correctly suggested that geosynchronous satellites would be useful for communications. These orbits, sometimes called "Clarke orbits," are at equatorial latitude and at the precise altitude above the earth (approximately 22,300 miles) that matches satellite orbit time with the earth's rotation time. Hence the satellites are stationary relative to the revolving earth (see figure 2–11).

Over twenty-four communications satellites are now in geosynchronous orbits, all at assigned longitudes for separation control. U.S. satellites are separated at 4°, but closer spacing is under study. Launches are becoming cheaper (especially with the space shuttle), as are components (for example, through the use of GaAs FET (gallium arsenide field effect transistor) solid state tranmitters). These satellites primarily carry telephone conversations, television broadcasts, text (both videotext and such newspapers as *USA Today* and the *Wall St. Journal*), and more recently, computer communications.

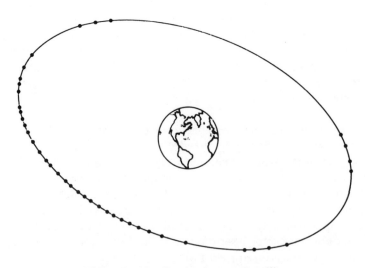

Figure 2–11. Geostationary Satellites

The transponding or reflection of computer data by satellites presents two major hazards to computer security that were not of major concern before the development of satellite technology. First, satellite signals are arriving on the ground over a large area or footprint covering generally thousands of square miles. This issue is especially serious in the case of geostationary satellites because of their high orbiting altitudes. Satellite signals can be picked up by unintended or unauthorized receivers. For example, a major concern for satellite TV is the relative ease with which pay-TV signals can be intercepted by TV "pirates." Interception hardware costs range from a little over a hundred dollars to a few thousand dollars. Some other knowledge (frequencies, format, times, and direction of pointing) are needed, but these are generally relatively easy to obtain.

The remedy is conceptually simple: the digital data can be encrypted or the analog data scrambled. However, encryption technology extracts penalties because encryption keys must be maintained and distributed and there are increases in costs and complexity. As a result, satellite transmission is less efficient than might be desired.

Theft of data is not the only concern. Data are also vulnerable to destruction or interruption because satellite transmissions and receptions are available over a large footprint. People intent on mischief, vandalism, or terrorism can broadcast energy (with a substantial but not impossible investment) into the satellite-receiving antenna, thereby creating noise that jams the receiver. The remedies are well known but require additional investment or power or both to protect the data.

Public and Private Lines

The nation (and much of the world) is linked by a mammoth network of telephone communication links. Few buildings or offices are very far from the nearest telephone. Although this utility is mainly intended for voice communication, interface devices containing modems (and, in many cases, acoustic couplers) provide for computer communications. Similar communication links have also been developed specifically for data transmission, such as the Western Union TWX and TELEX systems used for teletypewriter communication.

Cable communication systems are also becoming common, and in many cases they compete with telephone services. Both public data-access channels and dedicated channels are used to transfer television, communication, and data signals. These links were originally intended for broadcast communications from one source to any number of receivers. Now that point-to-point communication is required by increasing numbers of applications, security (restricting data transfer to intended locations) is becoming important.

Public and private communication links can be hard-wired, electro-magnetic terrestrial, or satellite. They are treated separately because of their pervasiveness, importance, and special security vulnerabilites. Available special services include WATS (wide area telephone service), private line or dedicated networks, DDS (digital data service), leased networks (AT&T, Western Union, MCI, Southern Pacific, ITT, RCA, and Satellite Business Systems, among others), and packet-switched networks (GTE Tymnet, Telenet, ARPA).

For nearly as long as public-line service has been available, people have devised methods to create passive taps for eavesdropping. Unfortunately, new technology such as microprocessors has made these techniques more powerful. Specific dialed numbers or groups of numbers can be selected; text or speech can be scanned for patterns of interest; data links can even be actively interfered with (data can be altered or inserted) without detection.

3 Software and System Constituents

Software and data are less visible components than computer hardware because they represent logical procedures and information as opposed to physical devices. However, the system software and data exist in various forms in the computer hardware devices. They also generate important computer-security issues because software and data control the computer-system operation. This section surveys some of the most important software and data components, particularly operating systems, compilers, firmware, applications programs, and data sources and storage.

Operating Systems

An operating system controls computer performance with as much autonomy as possible to minimize the inefficiency of continual human intervention. Operating systems receive human commands (through software or hardware), furnish operator prompts, and return diagnostic information, in addition to controlling program operation. Early computers had essentially no operating system. Some contemporary small computers and programmable calculators are also in this category. The operator of these systems is more intimately associated with the computer operation. However, any form of user interaction involved in computer operation is one of the most crucial factors in computer security.

There are two basic types of operating systems: batch and interactive. In batch operation, a program or sequence of programs is run from beginning to end (if not interrupted by fatal errors). Diagnostic messages may be generated, but they are delivered to the user after the fact, instead of suspending execution pending user analysis.

Interactive operating systems are mainly intended to accommodate users at remote terminals who are time-sharing the computer resource. The user typically interacts with the computer on a command-by-command basis as opposed to a program-by-program basis. Interactive operating systems are popular because they give rapid error-condition feedback and ease alterations. This ability to enter data or commands sequentially and get prompt feedback has given users new power and intimacy with the computer functions.

Modern operating systems handle more functions and are increasingly responsible for the logistics of communication between each of several (possibly simultaneous) users and particular portions of memory. However, it is becoming harder to ensure that user-data partitions are protected and that no possibilities exist for cross-connection of users and misrouting of data.

An operating system carries out several important functions for software routines which include: monitors, loaders, editors, and debuggers.

Monitors

Computer communication is centralized in the monitor. Console commands are directed to the monitor and it controls the execution of other subprograms. When several programs are running simultaneously on a computer, they are all under monitor control. The monitor typically controls the computer's interaction with peripheral devices such as printers.

There are several common types of monitors: single-job monitors, which control one job at a time; and foreground/background monitors, which handle programs as "priority" or "nonpriority," transitioning in response to the resources required.

Loaders

Programs are entered into the computer system with loaders. A bootstrap loader loads simple programs (including other loaders) into the proper memory locations. In addition to controlling loading locations, loaders typically check for errors during the loading process (such as reading data from tape). Relocating loaders can load various programs into nonconflicting memory locations, whereas absolute loaders are more constrained. Loaders can also establish the links that allow programs to refer to each other and can control references to library (system storage) data.

Editors

Additions, deletions, and other modifications to programs can be made during interaction with the operating system in most computers. The editor function is similar to the editing capabilities provided in word processors and word-processing software, but usually on a far more restricted scale. Editors use an accessible buffer area to temporarily store data for editing. When editing is complete, the buffer data can be staged toward a more permanent storage area or used in program execution.

Debuggers

Debugging routines provide break points for error isolation. Execution can be controlled to give the user intermediate feedback. Debuggers are written to enable as comprehensive an analysis as possible. Diagnostic messages regarding program features that will cause problems (or are causing problems) during execution are frequently provided.

Translators

There are several levels of software in a computer system, ranging from machine language and microprograms at the most intimate machine-instruction level, to high-level languages, which are intended to include abstractions (such as equations) and be user-friendly (written and organized in a way that is familiar and convenient for the user). A program written in a high-level compiler language (or in an interpreter language or even in an assembly language) must be translated to machine language before execution by a computer. The software routine that translates the language is called a compiler, interpreter, or assembler, depending on the input to the translation process.

Assembly language is intimately associated with the particular computer on which it runs. High-level languages (compilers) and interpreters are more generally oriented toward users. Translators are generally required for more than one high-level language for each computer. The translator code generally is not portable to most other computers, so the code generally is dedicated to a particular computer. Because a very crucial and complex software package (or packages) resides in the computer and is involved in every instruction executed by the computer, translators must be considered in addressing computer-security issues.

Firmware

Software that is committed to hardware (for example in ROMs) is called firmware. Firmware exists in mainframe computer-system control circuits, controller hardware (such as peripheral devices), switching devices (such as port contenders), and sometimes in coding devices (cryptographic keys).

Usually only the most dedicated software and that least likely to require changing is committed to firmware. This type of commitment decreases flexibility. Even ROMs, although they can be changed, are not nearly as flexible as read-write memory. However, firmware also has security implications. It is not as readily tampered with as is software. For this reason, it can be very important that crucial security-oriented software be placed in firmware.

Applications Programs

Operation systems and translators are utility software that make the computer system easier and more convenient to use. However, utility software can be likened to the circuits in a phonograph—you won't hear the music until you put the record (that is, the program) on.

Applications programs are generated by users to accomplish specific tasks. These programs can be dedicated ("production programs") or ad hoc (used at most only a few times for special purposes).

The security aspects of applications programs vary widely. Some programs handle large amounts of financial data, some access data that must be protected from unauthorized disclosure (such as classified, proprietary, or private information), and some control values for crucial processes (such as nuclear reactors and weapons). Security interests vary accordingly. A production program handling large amounts of money, for example, would normally be closely reviewed by computer security and EDP auditing personnel.

Information Base

The data on which programs operate is usually crucial to the computation process. Data can be stored using a number of methods, each of which raises unique and important problems for computer security.

A typical information base might be contained on magnetic disk (or possibly tape). Data are stored in a variety of locations and media. In addition, a disk or tape may reside in a library or special storage location for long periods before use. Information can also be kept in a formal database controlled by a database manager software system.

System Architecture and Component Technology

The technical strategies of designing and developing computers generally fall into two classes: architecture and component technology. Architecture is the term for the way that basic computer building blocks are put together to form a system. Component technology refers to the basic circuit components that are used to realize the system functions.

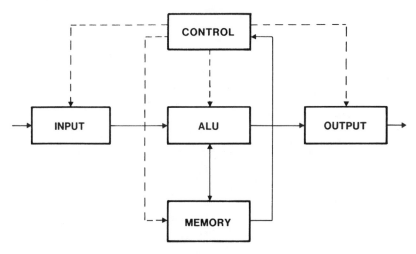

Figure 3-1. Basic Computer Architecture

Architecture

Figure 3-1 shows the classic simplistic architecture of a computer system. ALU is the arithmetic and logic unit, which performs such basic computer operations as add, subtract, multiply, divide, shift, and compare. The memory contains programs and data. Input and output are interfaces with the outside world. The control unit governs all operations. Many early computers were built according to this basic architecture, as are some of today's small computers.

The more sophisticated architecture in figure 3-2 allows peripheral activities involving input, output, and memory to take place in parallel with the main computing activity. The PDP/11 family and some models of the IBM System/370 use similar architecture.

Multiprocessors (computers using more than one processing unit) increase processing speed (figure 3-3). Computers based on multiprocessor architecture include the Univac 1100/80 series and the Burrough B5000. However, multiprocessor architecture requires either the user or the system designer to find efficient ways to take advantage of the parallelism.

Some computers (such as the CDC 6600, CDC 7600, some CDC CYBER 200 Series, and some IBM System/360 and 370 computers) perform multiple simultaneous operations from a single instruction sequence (see figure 3-4). Pipelining (figure 3-5) is used to speed up array processing

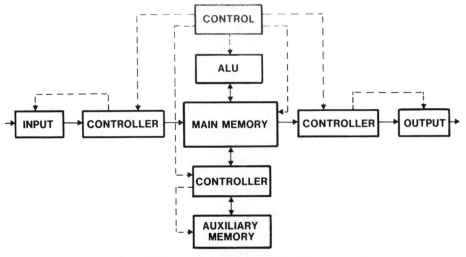

Figure 3-2. Computer Architecture with Peripheral Control

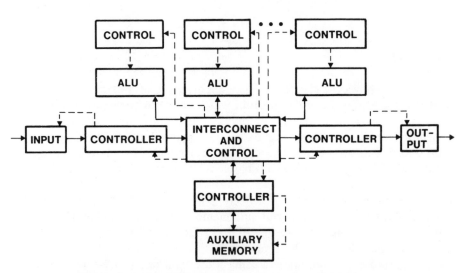

Figure 3-3. Multiple-Processor Computer Architecture

by operating on multiple array members simultaneously. The CRAY 1, which also uses vector processing (simultaneous operation on vector constituents), is among the computers using pipelining. Parallel processors act much like computers in parallel (figure 3-6). This strategy was used in the Illiac IV computer.

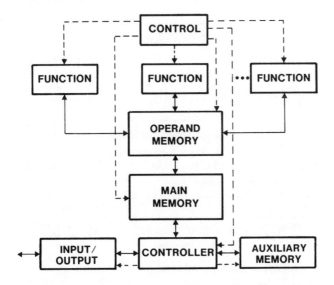

Figure 3-4. Multiple-Operation Computer Architecture

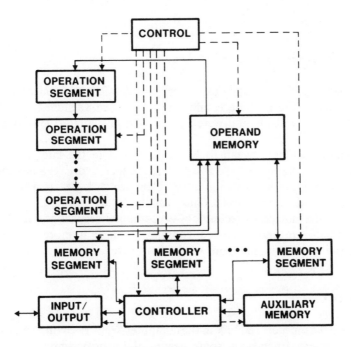

Figure 3-5. Pipelined Computer Architecture

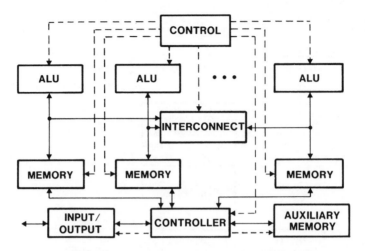

Figure 3-6. Parallel Computer Architecture

The new complex computer architectures make computer security measures more difficult to assure, because of the increased possibility for unusual performance features.

Component Technology

The earliest digital computers used electromechanical components (for example, relays). The first electronic computers used vacuum tubes. Transistors became available and were widely used in the late 1950s and early 1960s.

Integrated circuits began to be incorporated in the late 1960s. This technological evolution has led to smallar, cheaper, more reliable, and less power-consuming computer circuitry. New technologies (GaAs, supercooled semiconductors) show promise for the future.

One of the impacts of technology on computer security is that the high speeds, small size and increased complexity make it more involved to analyze the security implications of the hardware.

Computer Users

People are the most crucial link in the computer-security chain. The security of every system depends on some degree of integrity among the people accessing the system. Programmers of complex systems are usually so familiar with the intimate details of the system that it is essential that they be screened and trusted. Many users of a system have access to data that they are trusted not to convey to an unauthorized source (electronically or otherwise). Rules and procedures are set up for people to follow with the full understanding that some trust is necessary for the system to work. The bottom line is that most of the computer security performance features depend heavily on the people involved.

4 Protective Procedure-Based Techniques

This chapter addresses one of the three basic categories of computer-security measures—procedure-based techniques. Hardware protective measures are discussed in chapter 5, and software security routines are described in chapter 6.

Procedural requirements are the basis for several computer-security measures. These procedures include access controls for getting to and using computers; reading, writing, and manipulating files; handling computer-related documentation; tracking personnel behavior; and providing backup and recovery.

Computer Access Control

Access control procedures ensure that only designated individuals are allowed entry to a physical area, the use of a computer in a particular mode, or the use of specific data in computer memory. Typically, access is gained by testing something a person knows, something a person has, something a person is, or something a person is capable of doing. For example, passwords are commonly used for access control in computers. A user is given (usually by a system routine) or enters a unique combination of letters, usually in the form of a word. Only the user and the computer memory have a record of the password. The user is granted access on successful entry of the password. Another access procedure may require the use of an identification card (such as a bank cash card, which provides access to automatic tellers). However, such cards are almost always supplemented with some other form of identification.

Fingerprints are an example of something a person is. Fingerprints have been reliable and popularly used identifiers for many years. Something a person is capable of doing is a more difficult concept. It is fairly difficult to establish a unique characteristic in this class—for example the way a person talks, types, or walks.

Most computer-security procedures are based on something a person knows or knows how to do. For all techniques there are important measures of performance. An access-control system should be extremely reliable in properly granting access to authorized personnel and also in denying access to unauthorized personnel. The system should also be convenient, readily accepted by user personnel, and inexpensive.

Passwords

By far the most popular access-control technique is password control. Passwords are sets of numbers, characters, words, or combinations that must be entered into the system for access. Password systems provide a reasonable assurance that the password user is authorized to use the computer, and they facilitate accountability by identifying the user. Usually a "user identifiction" (name or unique number) is entered to indicate the user; the system then expects the user to enter a password and verifies the claim by matching the ID to the password.

In addition to IDs, the computer memory also includes password associations to other necessary data, such as the user's name, identification code, data access privileges, or accounting specifics. Because the passwords in memory represent information that must be protected, various forms of internal protection are required. Historically, passwords were assigned to both individuals and groups. However, in the last decade or so, the use of shared passwords has all but vanished, mainly because responsibility and accountability and security problems have increased substantially.

Several steps protect passwords as private information:

1. Users must be motivated to protect and not share their passwords. This motivation can be through training, threat of repercussion, and a clear explanation of the risks associated with compromise.
2. Passwords should be easy for users to remember, so that they will not be written down in accessible places. There are four basic ways to ensure that users can remember their passwords. First, passwords could be short. The security risks associated with this approach are obvious.

   Second, users could select their own passwords. Many computer-security managers prefer this approach because it not only reinforces the probability that the user will remember the password, but it also can be protected so that no one but the owner (not even system administrators) can observe it.

   Third, passwords can be made especially memorable—for example, by giving passwords phonetic characteristics. This approach (which I prefer) depends on structuring combinations of vowels, consonants, digraphs, and other features to generate pronounceable characteristics. This type of password is easily memorized and popular with users.

Fourth, memory can be reinforced by structuring the password as a phrase of known words that make sense (for example, "see the fox run"). Whatever technique is used, ease of memorization is an important requirement.

3. Passwords, should be changed regularly. Although degree of use, level of security requirements, and sensitivity of protected information are important factors, most computer-security professionals recommend routine password changes at least once a year, with more frequent changes encouraged in case of suspected compromise of user dissatisfaction.

4. Any records of passwords must be well protected. Such records include any written forms and computer memory records. Written lists should be minimized or eliminated. Computer memory should be inaccessible to all but trusted system administrators. Encryption (discussed in a later section) can obviate this concern.

5. Repeated unsuccessful password tries can indicate an attempt to bypass password protection. The computer can be programmed to recognize and combat such attempts by slowing down or disabling system-user communication and feeding back information to users and security personnel on successful log-in of the date and time of their previous successful log-in and the number of subsequent unsuccessful attempts.

6. Passwords should not be visible. Terminals and control screens should not display passwords. Most systems provide blanking for password entry, but if this is impossible, the screen should be protected from view. Password cards should not be interpreted or printed.

A key philosophy of password management is to match the password robustness to the degree of protection desired. That is, data requiring minimal protection (such as the phone directory of a company) or computers to which access restrictions are not important might be protected by two- or three-character passwords. On the other hand, some forms of protection must be very stringent, such as classified information (which requires that the passwords be treated at the highest classification level of the data protected) and passwords that enable control of funds transfers.

One way of increasing robustness is to increase the password length. For example, a six character password with each position chosen randomly from the 26 alphabetic characters and the 10 decimal digits has 36^6 possible forms. As a result, a randomly tried password has less than one in 2 billion chances of success. A seven character password with each position chosen from alphabetic characters has over 8 billion possible forms.

However, passwords that are too long to be easily memorized are inconvenient for users. They are consequently more likely to be compromised. Users of these passwords have a tendency to leave password issue cards in the vicinity of their work or to write passwords in insecure places (such as blackboards and desk pads).

Allowing users to select their own passwords is a controversial approach because users in general are not as security-conscious as those responsible for computer security. Commonly selected passwords are single letters, user names, user initials, user birthdate, spouse's or child's name, or other such personal—and accessible—information. Some problems can be prevented by designing the password software so that it accepts only passwords of at least a prescribed length (such as six characters). However, because a user might select six As, it is apparent that checks of user passwords for acceptable qualities are difficult.

Password phrases are generally more memorable than random-digit passwords, but there are disadvantages. The most important are that computer memory space for "passphrase" storage is larger and that users must spend more time entering a phrase than entering a word.

Phonetic (pronounceable) passwords are an effective compromise. Phonetic characteristics structure vowels and consonants into forms that approximate language construction. The most basic forms comprise consonants, vowels, consonant digraphs, and vowel pairs. However, there are no constraints that the words must be meaningful (for example, ZIGOFOO). This construction technique is analogous to "context-free" grammar in formal language construction. A phonetic password construction scheme can yield over 50 million seven-letter password possibilities.

A phonetic password generator (or any other type of password generator) can control access in two ways: either a central authority (password control organization or system administrator) issues passwords, or a user-called routine can generate random passwords. Users can be given the capability to reject any password and call the routine again.

Password management should also incorporate the following procedures:

1. Passwords should be disabled as soon as possible when computer-use authorization ends (that is, when a user is fired, transferred, or resigns, or when compromise is suspected). Special attention should be given to terminations under duress. A significant amount of damage is possible at the hands of disgruntled personnel whose computer access remains intact.

2. Passwords should be changed periodically. The time increment usually depends upon the access sensitivity, but once a year is usually the minimum frequency. Password changes decrease the probability that a password will eventually be compromised. Regular password changes also ensure that authorization can be conveniently reverified and bookkeeping can be updated (for example, changes in name or organization).

3. Users should be permitted and encouraged to obtain a new password any time a compromise is suspected or any time a password becomes cumbersome for a user (for example, hard to remember).

Algorithms

Algorithms (programmable routines) can be used in place of or in addition to passwords. The intent is to require the user to do prescribed tasks that only the identified person could do.

One technique is an access quiz. The system prompts the user for personal data that are theoretically known only to the person, such as a wife's maiden name, mother's birthday, or a pet's name. The questions are picked at random during the log-in process.

Another possible approach is to issue numbers to a user and require that a computation be made. For example three decimal digits, such as x, y and z, could be issued. During log-in, users could be given two random operators α and β to go with the three operand digits in the form:

$$x \, \alpha \, y \, \beta \, z$$

where α and β represent addition, subtraction, multiplication, and division. For example, a user with the issued digits 5, 1, and 8 might get an algorithm request during the log-in process:

$$x + y - z$$

The expected user response would be -2.

File Access

In addition to authorization to use a computer, access to files often requires security procedures. Files are generally identified by a file name. Knowledge of the name is necessary for user access. It is common to also protect the file from unauthorized access through file passwords and/or access tables.

File passwords and computer access passwords provide similar protection. An access table is a stored mapping relationship between users and their privileges. These access control techniques are based on the assumption that the user has already been validated. File access tests simply check what the user can do with files once computer access has been obtained. Because the use of files is generally controlled by file owners, user-selected file passwords are common. Sometimes, software controls are placed on file

| | File Partition: | | |
Job Partition	Secure	Administrative	Open
Secure	read/write	read	read
Administrative		read/write	read
Open			read/write

Figure 4-1.   Partition Access-Control Matrix

password length, but file passwords are generally not considered to be as critical to security as computer-access passwords.

Files can also be restricted by partitioning. That is, files may be separated into discrete segments, each with some common purpose. For example, a company's files might be partitioned as secure (classified or defense-oriented), administrative (payroll, purchasing, personnel), and open (unrestricted use). In a partitioned environment, file-access rules may depend on the partition in which the computer job is running and the partition from which the file was saved. The typical partition-access matrix in figure 4-1 illustrates how this control can be exercised. "Read" means a user in the indicated job partition can only read a file in the indicated file partition; "write" means a user in the indicated job partition can write or change a file in the indicated file partition.

User file privileges are diverse, depending on the particular computer system. They may include such operations as modifying, bestowing, writing, inserting, appending, reading, and executing.

"Modify" is an all-encompassing term for all changes that might be made in a single file or file directory (groups of file names listed in a directory tree hierarchy). "Bestow" allows a user to add authorizations for other users. A user should not be able to bestow rights unless the user already has those rights. "Write" privilege includes saving, replacing, deleting, creating a file name, updating the file data, adding descriptive information, among other privileges. Other possible rights may include directory removal, subdirectory and file addition, and directory descriptive information. "Insert" access is a technique to allow immediate descendant subdirectory additions. "Append" allows the user to add to descriptor file information. "Read" allows file transfer, copying, and descriptor listings, and sometimes directory descriptive information. "Execute" allows a file to be executed as a program.

Group access is a technique for file sharing. Any number of users from two to the world of users can be given file access. This technique is commonly used when a group of users are working with the same data or programs.

Personnel Communications

Communication with personnel (memos, messages) is an effective computer-security technique. It is not a technology, but strategies involved in training and structuring effective and comprehensive rules and procedures are an important adjunct to technology.

Rules and procedures cover a wide variety of topics: notification of restrictions to use computers for official business only; handling of passwords as private; handling and protecting computer output; methods for obtaining authorization to use computers; precautions to prevent unintentional electronic release of or tampering with computer data; control of personnel in the vicinity of computers, computer peripherals, or computer communication links; data classification rules; programming procedures; and software reviews and tests.

Most of these topics are elaborated on elsewhere in this book. However, if rules are to be effective, they must be reasonable and acceptable. Rules and procedures are relatively easy to circumvent, which reinforces the need to motivate users to attain effective compliance. One way to assess reasonableness in a quantitative fashion is to apply risk analysis (see chapter 6).

Training

Training in computer security is necessary; and effective if done carefully with cost-control measures. Awareness is important, but if overdone, the effort expended will be wasted. This section includes several examples of training techniques.

Memoranda to Users and Operators

Memos can be used effectively if they are kept short, concise, pertinent, and interesting. Memos can precisely define rules and procedures so there can be no doubt as to what is expected; give information on changes in systems or operations; convey general philosophies; and notify users of audits and reviews.

Visual Aids

Occasional group meeting programs on computer securtiy can be effective and interesting. Many movies, videotapes, and speakers are available that can address the general topic or specific incidents or aspects. These types of group meetings are useful for variety and because visual experiences are more readily remembered than written information.

New-Hire Orientation

It is common practice to introduce new employees to company policies, capabilities, and services during a new-hire orientation period or during new-hire orientation meetings. As the number of computer-assisted employee tasks increase, few if any employees will not be exposed to or responsible for computer operation. The orientation process provides a good opportunity for an introduction to computer security.

Patrol Scrutiny

Many companies have patrol personnel who scan work areas (especially after hours) checking for security problems. These security personnel can be assigned to look for exposed computer passwords. A careless computer user who writes a password on a desk pad or blackboard, or who leaves a password card on a table or desk, can be identified and given a warning or citation. Such reminders are effective mechanisms for increasing computer security awareness and encouraging users to protect private information such as passwords.

Newsletters

Computer security is an interesting topic to a wide spectrum of people, including computer users. Nationwide publicity on the topic has reached a large segment of the population. This basic interest can be a key to computer-security training. A computer-security newsletter can serve as an organ of company policy, can be used to publicize local- or national-interest incidents, and can be used for general philosophising.

Bulletin Board

A bulletin board dedicated to computer security provides an attention-focusing vehicle. Appropriate postings on such a device include news clippings with computer-security ramifications (incidents, laws, interpretations) and announcements (policy decisions and operational details).

Assistant Computer-Security Officers

A common structure for a company computer-security program is to place responsibility for the program in a single organization, usually either within the computing organization or within the security organization. However, distributed responsibility can enhance the program and provide a training mechanism. For example, the nucleus of program support could be assigned to a computer-security organization; and assistant computer-security officers could be appointed in computer-using organizations. This kind of distributed program has several advantages. Computer-security arms exist in close proximity to computer users, liaison between users and computer security is improved, motivation for meeting computer-security standards is improved, and training is enhanced in two ways: the computer-security organization provides information for the assistant computer-security officers and the assistant computer-security officers are a source of information for users. As a result, feedback from users to the computer-security organization increases.

Formal Procedures

The secure use of a computer, word processor, or other data-processing device does not happen by accident. Thought and planning and testing are important. The extent of the formal procedures depends on the complexity of the system and on the degree of protection necessary. Some important structured approaches to this problem are documenting security plans, conducting security reviews, and exercising operational systems using security tests.

Computer-Security Plans

A documented computer-security plan provides a record of the approach to be used to address computer security. The document is useful for reference by users, auditors, and computer-security officials. It provides a reference that transcends personnel changes. The capability to amend the plan ensures that it will be responsive to significant changes in equipment, operation, or personnel.

This plan should include specification of the hardware equipment, the software, the type of data, the physical locations and communication routes, and the local personnel responsible for computer security. It should also include specific security measures that apply to personnel (facility access, operational access, data access). Techniques for information security, communications security, physical equipment and access protection, and emanation security are important. The plan might also incorporate emergency procedures, contingency plans, backup provisions, disaster-recovery plans, and training procedures.

Computer-Security Reviews

The implementation of a system is a critical time. Usually, developers are more interested in achieving performance goals and operational status than in system security. When computer security is important, it is useful to conduct independent computer-security reviews by computer-security or EDP auditing personnel or both before the system becomes operational. These reviews are to check adherence to security policies and to provide comprehensive thinking about possible vulnerabilities or weaknesses.

Computer Security Tests

Actual tests of system-security features are important, even if the features have been carefully thought out, for several reasons:

1. Occasional discrepancies occur between designer expectations and system performance.
2. Sometimes a system is vulnerable to an unexpected mode of user behavior (intentional or accidental).
3. It is useful to assess how robust a system is and how weak its weakest links are.

Tests could include, for example, exercising standard security features, considering hardware/software failure modes, and identifying variations in hardware or operational status. Software, hardware, information, and physical security should be included.

Contingency Planning

One responsibility of computer security is to ensure that plans are made to back up critical hardware, software and data; emergency responses have been documented and roles assigned; and planning recovery from disasters achieves complete system operation in a minimum time.

It is not easy to plan for events that rarely happen and which no one wants to happen. However, in a thorough, well-conceived security program, the implications of disasters must be anticipated. Some events may be minor, some catastrophic. Contingency plans should cover the entire spectrum. Disasters can be caused by a long list of events: fire, smoke, or fumes; water damage (flood, rain, pipe breaks, drain blockages); earthquake; explosion; tornado or wind damage; electrical disturbances (lightning, power fluctuations, power failure, electromagnetic energy); air-conditioning failure or overheating; vandalism, terrorist attacks, or sabotage attacks on hardware; airplane, vehicle, satellite debris, or meteorite impact; chemical spillage; volcanic eruption; nuclear reactor disaster or other radiation effects; malicious software or data alteration or destruction; alteration or destruction of data by magnetic fields; personnel losses (death, sickness, strike); electronic funds theft; crucial errors by operating personnel; and catastrophic hardware failures.

It is important to establish backup procedures and plan for emergency response and recovery. Such contingency planning should include backup agreements, mutual-aid agreements, designation of responsibilities, prescription of steps, testing plans, and insurance as well as investigating replacement data communication modes (mail, courier, voice, leased lines, value-added, or packet-switching networks, and internal redundant lines).

However, there is a more technologically oriented approach to contingency planning. Several companies provide services that can be of significant value in recovering from disaster. For example, a computing capability service, or "hot site," is a fully equipped center that sells temporary computing capability. Equipment typically includes computers, disk drives, tape drives, and miscellaneous peripherals. Limits are imposed on both membership and length of use. Obviously, the computing capabilities of a hot center must be compatible with the member company's computers. Hot sites usually provide security, fire protection, power backup, and communications.

Another type of service is a shell facility or cold site. A recovery shell is designed to house a computing facility, but few if any CPUs. These shells usually provide power, cooling, raised floor, wiring, offices, and other physical facilities. Membership and length of use are typically limited.

Other types of services available from various suppliers include consulting, recovery management, matching companies with excess capacities with those needing backup and rapid facility implementation. In addition, companies should consider backup storage for various assets, including magnetic data tapes and disk packs, operating system tapes and disk packs, system documentation, program documentation, operating manuals and procedures, program source and object tapes or decks, forms, printer tapes, and wiring diagrams.

5 Protective Hardware Technology

Today, manufacturers offer a wide variety of hardware that provides useful computer-security functions. The major categories of such hardware are access control, information protection, and facilities protection. Such devices range from the very simple and inexpensive to the very complex and costly. Each of the devices described in this section could be used in at least some computer-security programs.

Access Control

One of the most interesting computer-security applications for hardware is the control of access to computers, facilities, rooms, terminals, data, or privileges (such as financial transactions). Such controls work in a variety of ways, but many involve biometrics (measuring something about one's body). These devices can control either access only or access and identification. Both functions require different performance characteristics and have different error rates. Access-only control, as its name implies, is intended to verify a person's right to access without specifically identifying an individual. For example, access-only hardware is used to control access to buildings, areas, or computer rooms. Identification controls determine the specific user for which access is to be allowed—typically, access to a computer for which use is individually accountable.

Several considerations govern the selection of the techniques and devices described in this section, particularly performance parameters. Some of the most important performance parameters for access-control devices are:

1. The probability of rejecting an authorized user should be very low. It is irritating and demoralizing for a user to be unjustly refused access. This type of error is generally caused by inconsistencies in the measurement process (typically the result of inconsistencies in the constituent being measured or the positioning of the object being read).
2. The probability of accepting an unauthorized user should be extremely low. The main function of access control, after all, is to minimize unau-

thorized usage. Generally, these errors occur because separability (finding unique features that characterize users) is very difficult.

3. Throughput rate should not be an operational bottleneck. That is, the time required to pass the barrier presented by an access control device should not be excessive. In addition, the time to register, enroll, or otherwise establish or update user records must be reasonable.

4. The memory required by the control (such as computer memory or device storage) must not be excessive.

5. System reliability must be acceptably high (long MTBF, or meantime before failure). An access-control system that does not function usually causes serious operational problems.

6. Maintenance must be reasonably straightforward. For example, it would probably be intolerable if a device had to be returned to the manufacturer for service.

Access-control devices range from the very simple (badges and locks) to the very complex (sophisticated biometrics). Their stability varies accordingly, both in the context of manufacturers and of products. For manufacturers of biometric devices, the current market is not stable and the techniques available are not generally well proved. As a result, some of the most technically interesting devices are not attractive from a marketing standpoint. Long-term financing depends on sales, and sales depend on competitive pricing and documented performance statistics. The synergy necessary to close the loop just has not yet developed for most of the sophisticated access-control devices. Nevertheless, the current technology warrants careful consideration. A considerable basis in technical work has been established, and some potentially powerful access-control devices have been built.

Fingerprint Analysis

Fingerprints have been used for over a century to identify individuals. Recently, automated devices have become available, and these identifiers have the potential to be incorporated in a computer-security program. Fingermatrix, Inc., for example, manufactures fingerprint recognition devices. The Fingermatrix equipment has been evolving, but currently relies on a 512-byte storage representation. Cost is about $6,500. The digital fingerprint data is derived during a scan while a person's finger is placed on a platen. Finger positioning is important and some time is required to complete a scan and process the data for comparison.

The identification is potentially reliable. Customer tests for failure to identify authorized users have been reported as low as 0.37 percent, with false admittance rate less than 0.03 percent. Not all user tests have been this successful, but the device is obviously promising. A "backup" fingerprint can be stored against the remote possibility that a finger with a bad cut or injury might not be recognized.

The access procedure typically requires identification of a user at a terminal connected to a host computer. The fingerprint data of the individual identified is retrieved from the host database and delivered to the fingerprint reader, where it is compared to the data being derived during the current scan.

Comparator Systems Corporation also makes a fingerprint-reading device. In its present form it is intended to be used to control computer access and to verify personal identity. It compares inked fingerprints to check a submitted print against a reference. Printak, Inc., is also working on a fingerprint recognition device.

Signature Analysis

Signatures are unique identifiers but forgery is possible. However, signature dynamics make signature identification significantly more reliable. While writing a signature, a person not only produces a pattern, but also makes a pressure deviation, acceleration, and time record that can be stored in an electronic identification system. Sandia National Laboratories, IBM, and Stanford Research Institute, among other companies, have begun research on this process.

Transaction Security Ltd. of England currently markets signature analysis devices, called VERISIGN II ® terminals. An electronic pen wired to the terminal is used to generate detectable electromagnetic energy, enabling dynamic tracking. The signature geometry and rhythm is digitized into a few bytes for storage on a magnetic-striped card. Storage (128 bytes) is also possible in a host computer. The acceptance threshold can be varied by adjusting sensitivity.

Another signature verifier is made by Micropad, Inc., for less than $5,000. Its device uses signature dynamics and senses motion through a resistance grid under the writing surface. A digitized representation (42 bytes) is stored in a host microcomputer. Any ballpoint pen can be used.

Palmprint Analysis

Like fingerprints, palmprints are unique to an individual. Palmguard Inc. is marketing an access-control system based on palmprint identification. In the PG 2000, a solid-state camera image is used to detect creases, skin tone, and swirls. The system provides fast (3sec nominal access time) and accurate (false reject rate < 1 percent) identification of individuals. The false acceptance rate is specified at 0.00025 percent. This extremely low rate is achieved with the aid of a keyboard number entry, which substantially increases the uniqueness measure.

To operate the PG 2000, the user enters an ID number on a keyboard. The system then prompts the user to place his or her hand in the jig. Correct hand position triggers a solid-state scanning camera (100 × 100 array of photo diodes) and the system transmits a 1,000-byte palmprint image to the computer for comparison with the image data recalled from internal memory. The authorized security officer, after being identified by the system, can add, delete or temporarily lock out users, or change access permissions (time of day, day of week) for each user. All user activity on the system can be recorded via an RS-232 output, providing time, date, and type and result of the user's activity. Output access control is provided in two forms—a DPDT hard-contact relay and an 8-bit encrypted parallel port.

The current PG 2000 is a standalone system intended for physical access control, but it can be adapted for computer database access control, cash-dispenser operation, and other applications. The basic system lists for $48,000. It has memory for 256 "handfiles." Palmguard has announced the new PG 2001, which is intended to be a "satellite portal unit" to sell for about $15,000. It will require a host (LSI 11/23) for profile storage.

Hand Geometry Measurement

Hand geometry identification is based on the length of four fingers on each hand, and on translucency of fingertips and webbing. The translucency measurements reportedly help to make forgery difficult. In a proven device developed by Stellar Systems that sells for about $5,000, hand geometry measurements are compared either with system-stored information or with information stored on a magnetic card that is the property of the user. The Identimat ® system can be used to control both single-point and multiple-site access. Access profiles of users can determine which locations they can access. A printer log records all activity.

Eye Blood-Vessel Patterns

The highly detailed and stable blood-vessel pattern of the retina of the eye, as well as its protected location in the body, make it a useful human descriptor for identification purposes.

EyeDentify, Inc., has developed a technology for low-level infrared scanning of the retina through a binocular eye camera. Sample reflected light levels are digitized and processed in a minicomputer and made available to access control systems, or virtually any other computer system, through a commonly used data communication link. The company offers a series of products to selected customers in a price range of $10,000 to $75,000.

Voiceprint Analysis

Characteristics of the human voice are detectable electronically and are difficult to imitate successfully. Voiceprinting has high potential as an access-control mechanism. Threshold Technology advertises a voice-analysis system, but field experience with the system is limited. Turnkey Information Processing, Inc., once marketed a voice-recognition product (Secure TIP®) that depended on translating and validating words into digital patterns for transmission to a host. Processing utilized discrete speech, speaker-dependent voice recognition. The imposter acceptance rate was advertised at less than 1 percent, and the MTBF was estimated to be greater than 10,000 hours. The voice processing depended on a 16-band filter bank for spectrum analysis and on recognition and verification algorithms. Adaptive features in the algorithms allowed for variations and temporary conditions such as colds.

Biometric Research

Other biometric research has explored using ear size and shape, facial structure, brain waves, electrocardiograms, blood characteristics, and lip patterns as access-control identifiers. Almost everyone in the access-control industry has heard the standard lip-pattern joke: one would arrive for work in the morning and have to kiss one's terminal to turn it on.

Coded Keys

In the recent past, magnetic-stripe cards have achieved widespread acceptance. They are used for electronic banking transactions throughout the United States and other countries. Although less well known, these cards are also used to control access to physical areas and terminals. Similarly, coded data on keys can keep authorized users from accessing computers. This technology offers the advantage of user familiarity with the keys as a locking device. In addition, such a coded entry device is somewhat disguised, looking like an ordinary key. Resdel Engineering Corporation has designed a coded access key that has the appearance of a house key, but stores about 16,000 bits. Datakey produces a similar device with storage in the 1,400 to 2,800-bit range that has the general shape of a key, but is not intentionally disguised.

Transmitters

Mastiff Systems produces "tokens," small low-power transmitters carrying coded intelligence. Mastiff tokens can be used as proximity-sensing devices to control physical entry. They can also be used to turn on terminals automatically when the user is near and disable when the authorized operator leaves the vicinity. The tokens are intentionally given limited battery power so they will not function more than a day if lost or stolen. Authorized users leave the tokens on the company premises after work, where they are recharged in a special-purpose high-security storage unit for use the next business day.

Cards

A wide variety of access control techniques depend on cards. Some of these are described here. The techniques have varying resistance to forgery (some self-erase if disassembly is attempted), but none are impervious. Individual cards are inexpensive (usually less than two or three dollars), but prices of complete systems range widely from $500 to $5,000 depending on their level of sophistication.

Photo Badge. A badge with a photo can be recognized by a guard or automatic visual system. Photo badges are commonly used for access control in conjunction with a guard force. These systems offer the advantages of simplicity, relatively low cost, and easy updating. The disadvantages center around human weaknesses such as inattention, recognition difficulty, and intentional disguise.

Magnetic-Spot Cards. Magnetic spots can be embedded in a laminated card to provide a unique identifier. Because typical densities are in the 40-spot range, the number of possible combinations is very large. Cardkey Systems and Rusco manufacture access magnetic spot cards.

Magnetic-Stripe Cards. Many companies make magnetic-stripe cards to control computer access as well as credit cards and bank cards. The magnetic field can vary from relatively low levels (300 Oersteds) to relatively high (40,000 Oersteds). EMIDATA Systems makes a permanently magnetized magnetic-stripe card.

Other Card Systems. There is a wide range of card techniques, some of which are described briefly in this section.

Electric-continuity cards use a printed circuit pattern to provide coded electrical continuity when inserted in a reader. Passive electronic cards, on the other hand, incorporate passive tuned circuits. When swept with rf energy, absorption as a function of frequency provides the code. Schlage Electronics makes passive cards that can be detected remotely at short distances (a few inches). Infrared optical cards (made by Continental Instruments Corporation and Secom among others) use ink that is opaque to visible light, but transparent to infrared. The code is detected by infrared photodetectors. Coded arrays of ferromagnetic wires can be laminated into cards (Wiegand effect) and detected magnetically.

Other card techniques include Hollerith (or other types of hole punching), bar coding, metallic strips for eddy-current sensing, and capacitance coding. The use of active electronic circuits (coded response with logic powered by transmitter) in controlling computer access has also been researched.

Locks

Access-control locks can range from standard key locks, spin combination locks, cypher locks (push-button combination), to such sophisticated devices as the Medeco twisting tumbler lock. Medeco claims that its twisting tumbler locks are "virtually pickproof" and that it offers several hundred times as many key patterns as for conventional locks. These locks operate like conventional locks for tumbler positioning, but utilize V cuts crisscrossing the key blade so that the tumblers rotate. The keys for these locks cannot be duplicated on conventional key-cutting equipment. Medeco sells a special key-cutting device and provides four levels of security.

Access locks of various types are available for computers, terminals, printers, and other peripheral equipment. One of these devices (Time-Lock Inc.'s Data Lock-100) is based on the Medeco twisting tumbler.

Silicon-Chip Cards

U.S. and foreign manufacturers have invested a considerable amount of development in "smart" cards containing a silicon chip, particularly to develop real-time money cards that carry account balances in RAM. The chip is structured to operate much like a microprocessor, including ROM and RAM functions. Transactions result in immediate updates. These cards also incorporate access-control features such as codes to recognize the authorized owner, logging user activity, and privilege mapping (restricting users to certain activities at certain locations).

Dial-up Control

Dial-up access to computers is a powerful resource for users and a potential threat to security. With dial-up capability, the computer can be used at home, in hotel rooms on a trip, and in remote offices. Theoretically, a user can access a dial-up computer from anywhere in the world a telephone connection can be established.

The price for this convenience is that it is difficult to restrict the telephone connection to authorized users. In numerous recent cases, telephone access by unauthorized users had done extensive damage to computer data resources. In some of reported cases, the major contributing problem was passwords with too small a population of possibilities. In other words, automatic equipment controlled by microcomputers was used to enter automatically passwords until successful access was made.

Such equipment has enormous power. For example, if attempts at access can be made and responded to in the typical time of 0.5 seconds, a microprocessor-based system could try 172,800 passwords per day. At this rate, it would take a little over 2.6 days to try all possible passwords for a system using four-character alphabetic passwords.

In addition to the procedures described previously (restricting number of incorrect access attempts for any connection and restricting the dial-up phone number), some manufacturers offer hardware technology to combat the threat. International Mobile Machines Corporation markets a control system called Privecode®, which screens calls automatically. One Privecode system can be applied to dial-up computers (Computer Sentry®), which answers with a synthesized voice, requesting a preassigned access code. No modem tone is communicated until the access code has been verified. Codes can be entered by voice or touchtone signals. The caller can use standard touchtone or rotary dial telephones.

A designated alarm threshold activates several response modes if invalid access attempts accumulate. In one mode of operation, only valid codes entered on the first try will be accepted. Subsequent correct or incorrect tries will result in a request for another try at entry. Another alarm mode response diverts the call to a security officer for trace initiation after a selected number (up to nine) of invalid tries. The caller is not aware of the diversion. Privecode also displays an alarm to an operator after a selected number of access attempts and deactivates the modem. Some recordings are displayed (accumulated invalid attempts, invalid codes tried). This type of protection costs about $1,500 per port.

LeeMAH, San Francisco, markets a device called a Secure Access Unit (SAU). It allows only authorized locations access to the dial file, by utilizing a call-back scheme. The SAU answers calls without any modem tone, thus masking the system from curious hackers. Users enter a six-digit location identification number, receive an acknowledgement and hang up. The SAU verifies the number and calls back; users then answer, enter a one-digit connection code and receive a modem connection. If a correct code is entered from an incorrect location, SAU calls the authorized location, thus thwarting the breach of security. The basic system provides for 100 authorized locations for under $1,000 per port. A multiport version serving up to 32 ports with more than 2,300 authorized locations has been announced. It has audit trail capability.

Such devices not only prevent searching for modem tones and making rapid-access attempts, but they also discourage tying up a port maliciously.

Miscellaneous Access-Control Devices

Several other techniques and devices have been used or considered for access control. For example, walking characteristics can form a unique individual pattern, as can terminal typing dynamics. Closed-circuit television maximizes observation powers and minimizes the number of required surveillance personnel. TV systems can be used to monitor unauthorized activity, check photo badges at remote entry stations, or videotape activity for later analysis. Current sophisticated equipment can operate at ultralow light levels and with automatic light compensation.

Intrusion-detecting alarms (for example, using sound, microwave, or infrared radiation), can be placed in secure areas where no personnel are authorized. Security switches have also been used to limit computer access, for example, by interrupting remote terminal connections to a host computer. Typically, such switches are placed in a technical control center and programmed to break the circuit connection during nonwork hours.

As another example of access-control technology, a writing-prevention ring is available for semimpermanent insertion in tape reels, replacing the write ring (which enables writing on a tape). If a write ring were accidentally or intentionally inserted in a reel of crucial data, the data could possibly be lost due to overwriting. The fiberglass-reinforced nylon ring (marketed under the name FILEGARD®) prevents the insertion of a write ring and does not activate the tape-drive write-enable switch. The ring can only be removed with a special tool.

Information Protection

The protection of information raises a host of considerations, depending on whether the information is stored in computer or peripheral memory or in user-readable documents, or whether it is transmitted through data-communication media. The protection hardware discussed in this section includes encryption hardware, error-correction and detection coding devices, electromagnetic-emanation shielding, and telephone-circuit protection devices.

Encryption Hardware

The ordinary transmission of computer data across standard communication links (wires, cables, telephone or other public lines, electromagnetic links, etc.) is formated according to well known transmission codes and protocol. Although an unintended interceptor of the information may not know the techniques used beforehand, experienced data-communications professionals can easily deduce the transmission/reception strategy. Therefore transmission codes are not considered encryption in the sense that they prevent the interceptor from deducing information that should not have been divulged.

Encryption, derived from the Greek word *kryptos* ("secret"), is the process of coding for secrecy (figure 5-1). Encryption has been used to disguise the content of information for centuries. Written and even spoken codes have been used in mystery stories, spy thrillers, and wartime applications. Edgar Allan Poe wrote a short story ("The Gold Bug") based on an encryption/decryption theme. Basically, encryption makes intelligence unintelligible to unauthorized observers. The level of encryption depends on the value of the information, how long secrecy is important, and the observer's perceived ability and motivation to decrypt.

Encryption was one of the many dramatic technological factors during World War II. The German Enigma encryption machine, the British Colossus computer work to improve decryption, and U.S. efforts to break Japanese and German codes all affected the outcome of the war—as well as the general development of computing and encryption technologies. Interest in encryption technology has now been rekindled as computing technology—particularly speed and power—has advanced and computing costs have declined. Cryptoanalysis has become enormously important; hence encryption techniques must be constantly improved.

A classic encryption method relies on code books of replacement characters or phrases. Managing code books however, is too cumbersome for a computing environment. Secret algorithms are not widely used because they can be discovered, possibly without the knowledge of the encrypter.

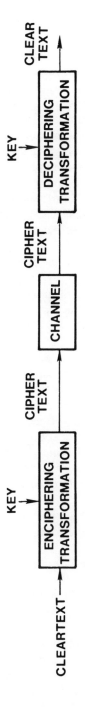

Figure 5-1. Basic Cryptographic System

Most modern cryptosystems use a key as an input to an algorithm (figure 5-1). The key must contain enough numbers to prevent discovery by trial and error—for example, exhaustive search of the key space. The algorithm must map as uniformly as possible onto the code space so that it gives observers no way to reduce the key space that must be searched. It is now common to consider that the algorithm need not be protected.

Some common applications for encryption are communication protection (voice or data), file protection (computer database), password protection, and message authentication (for example, a check for a valid source when requesting a financial transfer). Encryption also protects financial data, financial transactions, classified information, password files, security files, restricted programs, private data (such as salary, medical history, and criminal or arrest records); proprietary data, management-sensitive data, and inventory records.

Communication encryption can be done end-to-end across a communication channel (that is, the message is encrypted at its source and decrypted at its destination), or by link encryption (that is, decrypted and reencrypted at each node transversed until its destination). Encryption can be done in hardware, software, or a combination of both. Hardware encryption is described in this section.

There are some disadvantages to encryption. It is relatively expensive— hardware must be purchased or designed and built or a software routine must be written. Transmission efficiency may decline because of the computational overhead. More memory may be required to store encryption/ decryption routines. In addition, encryption of a data subset flags that information as having special importance, unlike steganography (the process of keeping the existence of the information secret as well as the information itself secret).

The three general classes of encryption hardware include the following:

1. Devices for enciphering classified information. These National Security Agency (NSA) approved devices are prescribed for any U.S. agency handling classified information.
2. Data Encryption Standard (DES) devices, the most popular type of encryption device in general use.
3. Public-key encryption devices, which have limited uses but provide some special advantages.

DES Encryption. In 1972, the National Bureau of Standards (NBS) asked for proposals for encrypting commercial computer-data traffic. Results were unsatisfactory, so the call was repeated in 1974. As a culmination of work on the Lucifer project, a proposal by IBM was published in 1975. Comments were satisfactory and the algorithm became a Federal Information Processing Standard in 1977. The algorithm is intended to be used for unclassified data (not affecting national security) and is strongly oriented toward a hardware implementation. Because NSA is the federal communications security agency, NBS invited NSA participation and comment. NSA concurred in adopting the algorithm as a standard for unclassified applications.

DES is a set of operations on data blocks consisting of 8-bit bytes. The algorithm encrypts a 64-bit plain-text input into a 64-bit encrypted-text output using a 56-bit key (from a 64-bit key word containing 8 parity bits).

The algorithm is publicized and DES encryption hardware is available on the market. The algorithm utilizes an initial permutation, 16 key-dependent manipulations, and a final permutation. Overall, the algorithm is nonlinear; however, it relies heavily on modulo-two arithmetic.

The basic structure of the algorithm follows the logic shown in figure 5-2. The initial permutation is shown in table 5-1. Each bit of the 64-bit input block is shown in the table as the right member of a pair. The left member of the pair shows the transposition resultant position. For example, bit 58 appears in position 1, bit 50 in position 2, and so on.

The resultant 64 permuted bits are treated separately as a left-most (first) group of 32 bits (L_0) and a right-most (second) group of 32 bits (R_0). There are 16 operations involving interchanges, modulo-two (exclusive-or) addition and a key-dependent function, f (figure 5-2). The function is applied to a right-most group of 32 bits R_{i-1} and a derived 48-bit key K_i. The 16 operations correspond to $i = 1, 2, \ldots, 16$.

The E process transforms the 32 bits of R_{i-1} into 48 bits using the E transformation shown in table 5-2. In addition to a basic permutation, 16 of the bits are utilized in two positions. For example, bit 1 of R_{i-1} appears in positions 2 and 48 of E, bit 4 appears in positions 5 and 7 of E, and so on.

The 48-bit result of the E process is broken into 8 6-bit segments, each of which are used in an S process to obtain 8 4-bit segments (figure 5-3). The S (substitution) functions are specified in table 5-3. The 6 input bits for each of the 8 S functions are numbered $b_1, b_2, \ldots, b_6$. The combination of 6 bits specifies a decimal number equivalent to a 4-bit binary number. These 4 bits are the output of the S function. The P permutation of figure 5-3 is specified in table 5-4, where the first bit of the output is the sixteenth bit of the input, the second bit of the output is the seventh bit of the input, and so on.

The key derivations shown in figure 5-4 involve left circular shifts and the functions $PC1$ and $PC2$. The input to the key derivation process is the 56 key input bits. (Bits 8, 16, \ldots, 64 of the 64-bit key are selected so that each byte has odd parity. These bits are discarded for the key derivation process.) The $PC1$ transformation on the 56 key bits is shown in table 5-5. The first output bit is bit 57 of the key, the second is bit 49, and so on. The first 28 bits of the output yield C_0 (figure 5-4); the second 28 bits provide D_0.

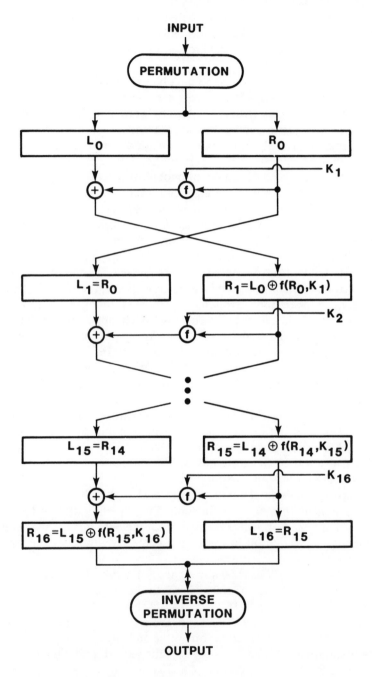

Figure 5–2. Basic DES Logic

Table 5–1
Permutation Table

1-58	17-62	33-57	49-61
2-50	18-54	34-49	50-53
3-42	19-46	35-41	51-45
4-34	20-38	36-33	52-37
5-26	21-30	37-25	53-29
6-18	22-22	38-17	54-21
7-10	23-14	39-9	55-13
8-2	24-6	40-1	56-5
9-60	25-64	41-59	57-63
10-52	26-56	42-51	58-55
11-44	27-48	43-43	59-47
12-36	28-40	44-35	60-39
13-28	29-32	45-27	61-31
14-20	30-24	46-19	62-23
15-12	31-16	47-11	63-15
16-4	32-8	48-3	64-7

Note: Permutation (left bit position for right bit number); inverse permutation (right bit position for left bit number)

Table 5–2
E **Transformation**

1-2,48	17-24,26
2-3	18-27
3-4	19-28
4-5, 7	20-29,31
5-6, 8	21-30,32
6-9	22-33
7-10	23-34
8-11,13	24-35,37
9-12,14	25-36,38
10-15	26-39
11-16	27-40
12-17,19	28-41,43
13-18,20	29-42,44
14-21	30-45
15-22	31-46
16-23,25	32-47, 1

Note: *E* transformation (32 bits to 48)

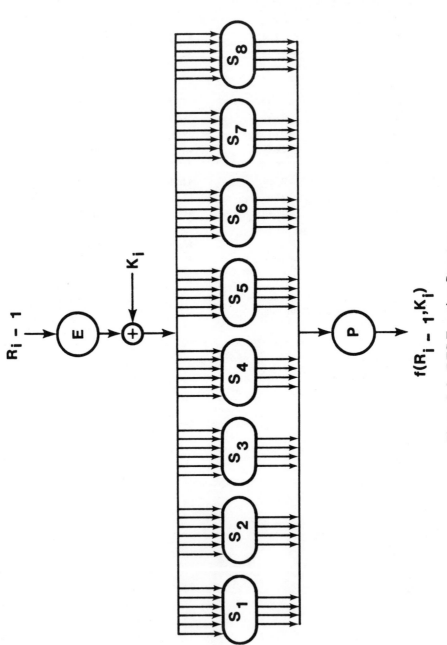

Figure 5-3. DES Function Structure

Table 5-3. Substitution Table

S_1 $b_2b_3b_4b_5$	0000	0001	0010	0011	0100	0101	0110	0111	1000	1001	1010	1011	1100	1101	1110	1111
b_1b_6																
00	14	4	13	1	2	15	11	8	3	10	6	12	5	9	0	7
01	0	15	7	4	14	2	13	1	10	6	12	11	9	5	3	8
10	4	1	14	8	13	6	2	11	15	12	9	7	3	10	5	0
11	15	12	8	2	4	9	1	7	5	11	3	14	10	0	6	13

S_2 $b_2b_3b_4b_5$	0000	0001	0010	0011	0100	0101	0110	0111	1000	1001	1010	1011	1100	1101	1110	1111
b_1b_6																
00	15	1	8	14	6	11	3	4	9	7	2	13	12	0	5	10
01	3	13	4	7	15	2	8	14	12	0	1	10	6	9	11	5
10	0	14	7	11	10	4	13	1	5	8	12	6	9	3	2	15
11	13	8	10	1	3	15	4	2	11	6	7	12	0	5	14	9

S_3 $b_2b_3b_4b_5$	0000	0001	0010	0011	0100	0101	0110	0111	1000	1001	1010	1011	1100	1101	1110	1111
b_1b_6																
00	10	0	9	14	6	3	15	5	1	13	12	7	11	4	2	8
01	13	7	0	9	3	4	6	10	2	8	5	14	12	11	15	1
10	13	6	4	9	8	15	3	0	11	1	2	12	5	10	14	7
11	1	10	13	0	6	9	8	7	4	15	14	3	11	5	2	12

S_4 $b_2b_3b_4b_5$	0000	0001	0010	0011	0100	0101	0110	0111	1000	1001	1010	1011	1100	1101	1110	1111
b_1b_6																
00	7	13	14	3	0	6	9	10	1	2	8	5	11	12	4	15
01	13	8	11	5	6	15	0	3	4	7	2	12	1	10	14	9
10	10	6	9	0	12	11	7	13	15	1	3	14	5	2	8	4
11	3	15	0	6	10	1	13	8	9	4	5	11	12	7	2	14

Table 5–3 continued

S_5

b_1b_6 \ $b_2b_3b_4b_5$	0000	0001	0010	0011	0100	0101	0110	0111	1000	1001	1010	1011	1100	1101	1110	1111
00	2	12	4	1	7	10	11	6	8	5	3	15	13	0	14	9
01	14	11	2	12	4	7	13	1	5	0	15	10	3	9	8	6
10	4	2	1	11	10	13	7	8	15	9	12	5	6	3	0	14
11	11	8	12	7	1	14	2	13	6	15	0	9	10	4	5	3

S_6

b_1b_6 \ $b_2b_3b_4b_5$	0000	0001	0010	0011	0100	0101	0110	0111	1000	1001	1010	1011	1100	1101	1110	1111
00	12	1	10	15	9	2	6	8	0	13	3	4	14	7	5	11
01	10	15	4	2	7	12	9	5	6	1	13	14	0	11	3	8
10	9	14	15	5	2	8	12	3	7	0	4	10	1	13	11	6
11	4	3	2	12	9	5	15	10	11	14	1	7	6	0	8	13

S_7

b_1b_6 \ $b_2b_3b_4b_5$	0000	0001	0010	0011	0100	0101	0110	0111	1000	1001	1010	1011	1100	1101	1110	1111
00	4	11	2	14	15	0	8	13	3	12	9	7	5	10	6	1
01	13	0	11	7	4	9	1	10	14	3	5	12	2	15	8	6
10	1	4	11	13	12	3	7	14	10	15	6	8	0	5	9	2
11	6	11	13	8	1	4	10	7	9	5	0	15	14	2	3	12

S_8

b_1b_6 \ $b_2b_3b_4b_5$	0000	0001	0010	0011	0100	0101	0110	0111	1000	1001	1010	1011	1100	1101	1110	1111
00	13	2	8	4	6	15	11	1	10	9	3	14	5	0	12	7
01	1	15	13	8	10	3	7	4	12	5	6	11	0	14	9	2
10	7	11	4	1	9	12	14	2	0	6	10	13	15	3	5	8
11	2	1	14	7	4	10	8	13	15	12	9	0	3	5	6	11

Table 5–4
P Transformation

1-16	17-2
2-7	18-8
3-20	19-24
4-21	20-14
5-29	21-32
6-12	22-27
7-28	23-3
8-17	24-9
9-1	25-19
10-15	26-13
11-23	27-30
12-26	28-6
13-5	29-22
14-18	30-11
15-31	31-4
16-10	32-25

Note: P transformation (32-bit permutation)

The $PC2$ transformation in figure 5–4 is specified in table 5–6. The 48-bit key derivation is determined by the 56 bits from the C and D processes. The result is that bit 14 of the CD pair becomes bit 1 of K_1. The left circular shifts applied to C_i and D_i for $i = 0, 1, \ldots, 15$ are specified with one shift for $i = 0, 1, 8$, and 15, and two shifts for the other twelve i.

The final inverse permutation of figure 5–4 is specified by the inverse application of table 5–1. That is, bit 1 of the final output comes from bit 40 of the $R_{16}L_{16}$ pair (R_{16} provides the first 32 bits; L_{16} provides the second 32), bit 2 of the output comes from bit 8 of the $R_{16}L_{16}$ pair.

The deciphering process is identical to the enciphering process, using the same key and the same algorithm steps. However, the identical key blocks used during encryption must be applied in the same order to the data. That is, K_{16} is applied first, K_{15} second, and so on.

The two basic types of DES encryption are common: the codebook mode and the cipher feedback mode (figures 5–5 and 5–6). The codebook mode enciphers 64-bit blocks independently. Although this approach is the simplest, it has the disadvantage of always coding the same message the same way unless the key is changed. Cipher feedback encryption feeds back some number of code bits (8 in figure) sequentially to a 64-bit shift register. The contents of the shift register are encrypted and the selected number of bits is added (modulo-two) to the input to obtain ciphertext. Decryption fol-

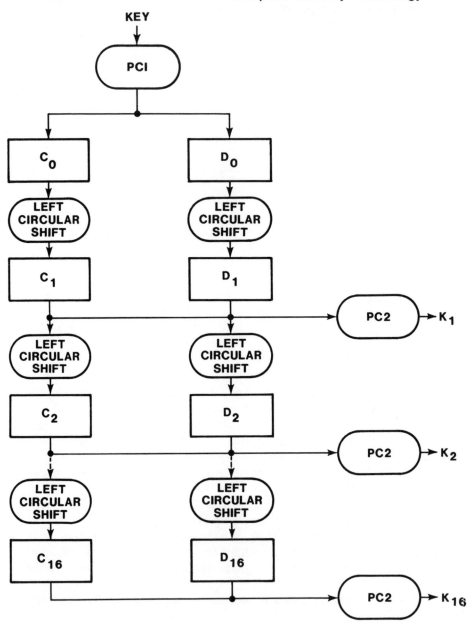

Figure 5–4. Key-Derived Functions

lows a similar process. Various other embellishments are possible, including block chaining (mixing bits from a previous ciphertext block with the cur-

Table 5–5
PC 1 **Transformation**

1-57	15-10	29-63	43-14
2-49	16-2	30-55	44-6
3-41	17-59	31-47	45-61
4-33	18-51	32-39	46-53
5-25	19-43	33-31	47-45
6-17	20-35	34-23	48-37
7-9	21-27	35-15	49-29
8-1	22-19	36-7	50-21
9-58	23-11	37-62	51-13
10-50	24-3	38-54	52-5
11-42	25-60	39-46	53-28
12-34	26-52	40-38	54-20
13-26	27-44	41-30	55-12
14-18	28-36	42-22	56-4

Note: PC 1 transformation (56-bit permutation)

Table 5–6
PC 2 **Transformation**

1-14	13-23	25-41	37-44
2-17	14-19	26-52	38-49
3-11	15-12	27-31	39-39
4-24	16-4	28-37	40-56
5-1	17-26	29-47	41-34
6-5	18-8	30-55	42-53
7-3	19-16	31-30	43-46
8-28	20-7	32-40	44-42
9-15	21-27	33-51	45-50
10-6	22-20	34-45	46-36
11-21	23-13	35-33	47-29
12-10	24-2	36-48	48-32

Note: PC 2 transformation (48-bit permutation)

rent plaintext block), and cipher block chaining (similar to cipher feedback except that an entire block of ciphertext is fed back).

Other modifications are sometimes made because while DES is basically a two-way symmetric cryptosystem, it is sometimes necessary to ensure one-way encryption (such as for password encryption). In contrast to the careful matching of encryption and decryption steps normally used for message transmission, decryption is sometimes not necessary—for example, in

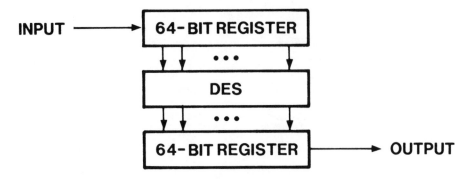

Figure 5-5. DES Codebook Encryption

password encryption. Passwords are encrypted to disguise their cleartext version, but never need to be deciphered. Password matching is as effective when encrypted versions of passwords are compared as when cleartext passwords are compared.

Another common DES modification used in many cryptosystems involves key variation. One way to ensure private communication and to reduce the possibility that enciphering keys will be discovered by continually monitoring transmissions (ciphertext attack) is to use session keys. A session key usually is considered to apply only during a single transmission connection. Each session will use a randomly selected key. For example, one session-key system depends on a master key to transmit the initial session key. However, the master key is used only to exchange a randomly selected session key for each session operation.

DES is the most common (but certainly not the only) encryption scheme available in commercial hardware. At least 28 companies now market data-encryption hardware; 14 include DES encryption as a central or only encryption technique. The performance characteristics of such hardware vary widely across such parameters as encryption speed, physical security, encryption enhancements, key management, cost, operational complexity, and physical configuration:

1. Encryption speeds range from 9.6 Kbps to 10 Mbps. Most devices operate near the lower end of this range; high-speed devices are generally the most expensive.
2. The price range per unit (two required for a link) ranges from about $300 to over $10,000. Encryption chips are available at a lower price; the quoted prices are for complete OEM boards or units.
3. All but the simplest units provide coding enhancements such as cipher feedback.

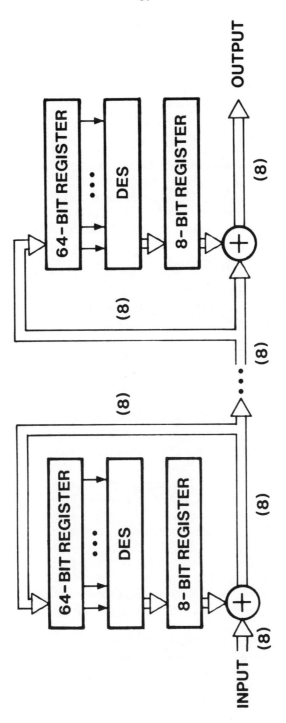

Figure 5-6. Example Cipher Feedback Encryption

4. Power consumption ranges from about 10 W for the least complex units to about 100 W for the higher-speed, more sophisticated products.

5. Key loading includes permanent embedding of a master key in some units; thumbwheel or other manual entry in some; reading code from a PROM-type physical key; and electronic key generation and loading. At least one unit uses public-key encryption (described later) for master-key loading. Session keys are frequently used with automatic session-key generation.

Although extremely popular, DES encryption is somewhat controversial. One reason is the relatively small key size ($2^{56} \approx 7.2 \times 10^{16}$). It is possible to build a special-purpose computer capable of checking all keys within days; however, it would cost tens of millions of dollars, although techniques like cipher-block chaining make this kind of code-breaking generally unattractive. NSA's involvement in DES has also raised fears that DES was tailored to a complexity level that could be broken by NSA. Others conjecture that some DES properties will eventually lead to a shortcut in breaking it.

Key management is another problem. Two stations can communicate with each other only if they have the same key, which raises management issues, especially if the stations are separated by long distances or if other logistic problems are associated with sharing keys. As a result, public key cryptosystems have recently attracted interest.

Public-Key Encryption. Key management is a concern in any cryptosystem. The most sophisticated encryption schemes are vulnerable if the keys are not carefully protected. Because key protection depends on individual vigilance and communication, key management warrants considerable attention. For example, keys should be periodically changed to avoid the possibility that a key will be compromised. If keys are delivered in written form, the storage or destruction of the key material is important. Physical security of these records under lock and key is essential. Reliable operations usually require backup storage of keys.

If communication nodes are widely separated, key transmission is a concern. The conveyance of keys by mail, courier, electronic links, or voice may result in exposure, possible delays, and reliability concerns. Finally, everyone sharing common keys can obtain information from other users, whether intended or not. For this reason, keys should be restricted to small groups. For large groups, the potential pairwise combinations grows impressively ($n(n - 1)/2$ for n members).

Although it does not sound plausible that two users could agree on an encryption key using public communication, Diffie and Hellman (1976) have shown that it can be done. Their approach, based on computational difficulty, uses finite field concepts. A field can be formed by using basic addition and multiplication operations modulo a prime number (a prime number is divisible only by itself and one). The modulus concept means that only the p integers $0, 1, \ldots, p - 1$ (where p is the prime number) are operands or results. If ordinary addition or multiplication gives a result outside this range, the result is divided by p and the remainder is used.

The following steps are illustrative in demonstrating a public-key encryption process:

1. User A selects a public prime number p and randomly selects an integer X_A in the range 0 to $p - 1$. User B picks a random integer X_B in the same interval. Both also use a public constant C.
2. A sends $Y_A = C^{X_A} \bmod p$ to user B. B sends $Y_B = C^{X_B} \bmod p$ to user A. Both Y_A and Y_B can be computed from X_A and X_B. However, the inverse (computing X_A and X_B from Y_A and Y_B) is very difficult if large prime numbers are used.
3. The session key for users A and B is computed as:

$$K = C^{X_A X_B} \bmod p$$

This computation is easy for both users because

$$K = Y_B^{X_A} \bmod p = Y_A^{X_B} \bmod p$$

In general, public-key encryption requires a public-enciphering transformation (with a public key) and a private-deciphering transformation (with a private key). The concatenation of the two transformations is used to recover the messages. A transmission sent with the recipient's public transformation can be deciphered only with the recipient's private transformation.

Secrecy and authenticity are both possible. The previous illustration provides secrecy because the key is not easy to find. However, any user could have initiated a communication with B in the manner shown for user A. User B has no way of knowing that user A was the source. Authenticity can be provided by having individual enciphering and deciphering transformations. That is, if user A wishes to send an identifiable message, the message is transformed using the sender's private transformation. The recipient uses the sender's public transformation to verify the authenticity of the message. However, in this case, the message is not secret because any recipient can use the sender's public transformation.

Public-key encryption schemes based on knapsack techniques can be used for secrecy but not for both secrecy and authenticity. (It is possible to achieve authenticity without secrecy in at least one trapdoor knapsack scheme.) The RSA encryption technique is a public key encryption technique that can be used for both secrecy and authenticity.

In 1978 Merkle and Hellman proposed a knapsack scheme for public-key encryption. A knapsack problem is essentially one in which choices must be made from a number of constituents to fill a receptacle precisely. Simple knapsack problems can be transformed into "trapdoor knapsacks" that are hard to solve without additional information.

For example, consider a set of positive integers, $P = a_1, a_2, \ldots, a_n$ and a number S that is the sum of some undefined subset of P. A knapsack problem is a simple knapsack if the set of elements is a superincreasing sequence (each element is larger than the sum of the preceding elements).

In the well-known algorithm for a simple knapsack solution, the elements can be checked one at a time. Merkle and Hellman gave a transformation that could be used to convert a simple knapsack into a trapdoor knapsack using modulo arithmetic.

In this system, the trapdoor knapsack corresponds to a public key and the simple knapsack corresponds to a private key. A sender desiring secrecy applies the intended recipient's trapdoor knapsack. The recipient is the only one who has the corresponding simple knapsack solution.

Consider a simplified example. Assume the simple knapsack set is:

$$P = \{1, 3, 5, 10\}$$

Also assume that the trapdoor knapsack uses two integers $u = 20$ and $w = 7$ such that their greatest common divisor (gcd) is 1 and $u > \Sigma \ p_i$ (elements of P). The multiplicative inverse of w in the modulo u system is 3. Assume that the message to be transmitted is $M = 1101$ (n binary digits). The transformation on P is:

$$P' = wP \bmod u$$

Then, the trapdoor knapsack (public key)

$$P' = \{7, 1, 15, 10\}$$

An inner product of the message treated as a vector and the P' set treated as a vector yields the code:

$$C = (1, 1, 0, 1) \cdot (7, 1, 15, 10) = 18$$

The recipient uses the transformation:

$$C' = w^{-1}C \bmod u$$

which is also equal to the inner product of of P and the message vector. This yields 14. The simple knapsack problem is:

$$14 = M \cdot (1, 3, 5, 10)$$

The solution to this simple knapsack problem is to select the elements of P from right to left so that the accumulated sum does not exceed 14. Because the fourth, second, and first elements are selected, the transmitted message must have been 1101. Only the recipient knows the simple knapsack set.

Graham and Shamir independently developed a similar trapdoor knapsack technique that is apparently more effective than the Merkle-Hellman scheme. In this process, each p_i (element of vector P) has a partitioned construction:

$$p_i = (R_i, I_i, S_i)$$

where R_i and S_i are long random-bit strings; I_i has length n with the ith high-order bit equal to 1 and the remaining $n - 1$ bits equal to 0. Each S_i has $\lceil \log_2 n \rceil$ 0s in its high-order bit positions to prevent overflow during summing. (The symbol pair $\lceil \rceil$ indicates "integer part of fractional parts rounded up.") A coding $C' = PM$ becomes:

$$C' = (R, M, S)$$

where

$$R = \sum_{i=1}^{n} R_i m_i$$

and

$$S = \sum_{i=1}^{n} S_i m_i$$

The elements of p_i without R_i and listed in reverse order yield a simple knapsack vector. R_i obscures the superincreasing property.

A trapdoor-knapsack vector P is transformed as in the Merkle-Hellman scheme (picking u and w as before) and computing $P' = wp \pmod{u}$. A message M is enciphered $C = P'M$, as in the Merkle-Hellman scheme. C is deciphered as $C' = w^{-1}C \bmod u$. However, the message can be extracted directly from C'.

In 1982, Adi Shamir proposed a polynomial time algorithm for breaking the basic Merkle-Hellman public-key cryptosystem. The attack addresses only the "single-iteration" Merkle-Hellman cryptosystem. Furthermore, as Shamir, Brickell, Davis, and Simmons have pointed out, there are countermeasures against the attack. However, Shamir's results have caused great consternation among many of those depending on the knapsack approach. In addition, recent attacks have revealed additional weaknesses in knapsack-based systems, including that of Graham and Shamir.

Rivest, Shamir, and Adelman published an encryption technique in 1978 known as the RSA public-key cryptosystem. During the time that public-key encryption has been studied, the two most widely assessed and used systems have been the knapsack technique and the RSA technique.

The basic encryption operation using RSA is:

$$C = M^e \bmod n$$

where the pair (e,n) is the public-encryption key, M is the message, and C is the cipher. Deciphering is done as:

$$M = C^d \bmod n$$

where d and n provide the key.

The enciphering and deciphering transformations can utilize fast exponentiation algorithms based on Euler's generalization of Fermat's theorem. A requirement for parameter selection is that

$$ed \bmod \phi(n) = 1$$

where $\phi(n)$, the Euler totient function, is the number of positive integers less than n and relatively prime to n. Here, n is chosen to be the product of two large primes (p and q), and $\phi(n) = (p-1)(q-1)$. An additional requirement is that M is less than n and that the gcd of M and n is 1 (M and n are relatively prime). The pair e,d is selected by knowing $\phi(n)$ and computing the inverse to obtain the other (because $ed \bmod \phi(n) = 1$). The pair (n,d) is the private key.

An extremely useful property of RSA encryption is that enciphering and deciphering are cummutative as well as mutual inverses. Because of this symmetry, RSA encryption can be used for secrecy and authenticity if to do so, senders encipher with their private transformations and then apply the recipient's public transformation. Recipients first apply their private transformation and then the sender's public transformation.

Using hardware of comparable complexity, public-key encryption is about three to five orders of magnitude slower than conventional methods such as DES. As a result, DES is much more popular commercially than public-key cryptosystems.

Error Correction, Detection, and Authentication Codes

Error-correcting and -detecting codes are important in computer security because they can provide data integrity and authentication during transmission. Both are accomplished by adding redundant information in the form of parity or checksum bits.

The basic operation used is exclusive-or or modulo-two addition—a special case of Galois field arithmetic $GF(p)$. The basic operation of this form is to perform addition and multiplication modulo a prime number. If the prime number chosen is 2, the addition is exclusive-or addition.

The most generally used error-correcting and -detecting (and authentication) codes use extension Galois fields $GF(p^m)$, where p is a prime number (usually 2) and m is the degree of an irreducible polynomial over $GF(p)$.

To illustrate one of the wide variety of techniques used in error-correction and -detection coding, consider a generator polynomial $g(x)$ of mth degree over $GF(2)$ with roots in the extension field $GF(2^m)$. The root structure is the designer's guide in selecting a polynomial with the desired performance. If the information bits to be encoded are thought of as coefficients of a message polynomial, coding is performed by multiplication over $GF(2)$ of the message polynomial by the generator polynomial. This yields a code polynomial, $c(x)$:

$$c(x) = m(x)\,g(x)$$

During transmission of the bit stream (corresponding to the code polynomial) through a communication channel (for example, over a telephone line, through a satellite link, or into and out of a memory medium), bits may change, converting $c(x)$ to $c'(x)$, which has the potential to be different from $c(x)$. Decoding is based again on $g(x)$, and again there are a variety of techniques. The simplest illustration would be in error detection, where division of $c'(x)$ by $g(x)$ determines whether any errors can be detected, based on whether there is a remainder in the division process.

$$\frac{c'(x)}{g(x)} = m(x) + 0 \text{ remainder} \;\rightarrow\; \text{no detectable errors}$$

Authentication and data integrity can be checked in a variety of ways. For example, the user can encode with a generator polynomial and test the received result by dividing by the generator polynomial. This process will result in high degree of confidence in the correctness of the process if there is no remainder in the division process.

Electromagnetic Shielding, Coupling, and Interference

Those who are not well versed in electromagnetic theory often naively assume that electrical signals are confined to electrical conduction paths such as wires, circuits, or CRT tubes. Unfortunately for computer security, not only does energy escape from the intended signal paths, it also can reenter unintended conductors such as other wiring, antennas, or fortuitous conductors, offering the potential for surreptitious and passive interception of intelligence. Such problems are generally described as emanation, coupling, or—in the case of classified information—the unclassified term "Tempest."

Nor is the coupling process unidirectional. Energy from such sources as motors, generators, car ignitions, and radio broadcasts can enter and interfere with data-signal paths and data-processing circuitry. Problems of this type are called interference, RFI (radio-frequency interference), EMI (electromagnetic interference) or intentional "jamming."

Interference with other systems can be illegal. Data-processing and communications systems are subject to FCC regulations, which have been troublesome to designers for the past few years. Now new FCC regulations, effective October 1, 1983, further restrict emanations. Several techniques can be used to combat problems of this type, ranging from the very inexpensive to the very expensive. The selection of any one approach depends on the data, the effects of compromising those data, the percentage of time that critical data are transmitted, the energy level of the intelligence, and a number of other factors. Obviously, the vulnerability of transmissions involving national security raise the highest concerns.

There are several preventive measures, including using low-level signaling. The higher the voltage and current swings, the greater the emanation potential. Emanations are also a function of signal-level transition time. However, performance pressures for high-speed transmission make this parameter less accessible to designers. Bandwidth restriction however, is part of low-level signaling. In addition, emanation sources can be separated from an unintended recipient or from wiring or fortuitous conductors that could carry information to an unintended recipient. The largest separations should be maintained between the strongest emanators and the most efficient receptors (such as CRTs and telephones). This issue is the basis for red/black separation rules for classified data processing and transmission, as well as the common practice of keeping emanators of critical data well within controlled areas.

Shielding circuitry and cabling can also protect data from electromagnetic emanations. The simplest, widely available form is shielded cable. Usually layers of conductors are braided (braided shield); solid shielding or conduit may also be used.

Shielding is more difficult within hardware devices. Because CRTs send out strong emanations, terminals, work stations, and personal computers may need to be shielded in some manner. Many manufacturers produce "Tempest-approved" equipment that meets rigid standards for minimal emanation.

Room (or similar volume) shielding has traditionally been a tedious and expensive process because high-frequency emanations can escape through incredibly small cracks in the shielding. Shielding around a doorway is taxing, especially as time passes and the sealing around the door begins to wear. Fortunately, however, any signal attenuation is helpful, and lower degrees of room shielding are now available through such low-cost techniques as spray-on conductive material. Incidentally, shielding works both ways. Not only does it confine or attenuate emanations, but it is also useful in reducing received interference. Fiber-optics transmission links have no useful electromagnetic emanations and cannot be interfered with through radiated energy. For this reason, fiber optics can be an effective technique for restricting emanations.

Jamming is also a potential method of interfering with data, particularly in electromagnetic links, such as microwave, terrestrial radio, or satellite transmissions. Little can be done to prevent energy from interfering with the links' receiving antennae. However, the effects of the jamming energy can be mitigated, making it prohibitively expensive to create debilitating jamming. For example, high-signal energy and high detection thresholds force the jammer to put more power into the attack at correspondingly higher expense. Another technique is to use a spread-spectrum bandwidth transmission, in which the electromagnetic link is not confined to a single frequency, but is distributed over a band of frequencies. The price paid is that the link components (the antenna, transmitter, and receiver) cannot be tuned to a single frequency. The payoff is that jamming energy must be spread over the entire spectrum. A variation is the use of frequency agility, where the transmitter frequency changes randomly over a spectrum, which again forces higher cost of effective jamming.

Data energy that inadvertently couples onto telephone, power, or other lines can frequently be attenuated or stopped before reaching unauthorized personnel with filters, transformers, and disconnects. Because data-transmission signals are usually conveyed at much higher frequencies than telephone or power, low-pass filters are effective. Power transformers provide adequate common-mode rejection and filtering to eliminate coupling at low frequencies (up to the 100kHz region).

Switches, disconnects, and insulating sections can be used in place of the conducting medium. For example, air conditioning or pipes can be interrupted with nonconducting segments. Telephones can use ringer regenerators and automatic disconnects so there is no continuity in the telephone

circuit when it is not in use. When the circuit is in use, the automatic disconnect is bypassed.

Grounding is of some interest in confining intelligence-bearing currents
because grounding pipes, wires, and ducts can carry currents outside a protected area. For this reason, single-point grounding (insofar as practical) in
the immediate vicinity of the data-processing equipment is desirable.
(Ground in this sense does not mean connection to metal such as water
pipes, but rather connection to "earth ground"—moist earth or other low-
resistance-to-earth-ground path.)

Some commercial data-processing equipment has been certified by
NSA-approved test procedures and appears on the Preferred Products List
(PPL) published by SCOCE (Subcommittee on Compromising Emanations). This equipment has extremely low emanation energy and is frequently advertised as "Tempest-approved." Although "Tempest-protected" equipment is also advertised that reduces emanations, "Tempest-
protected" is not synonomous with "Tempest-approved."

Direct Electrical Effects Protection

Computers and data-processing equipment are also subject to direct electrical hazards, from lightning, power transients, static discharges, and local
transmitters. Lightning protection has been studied seriously since at least
Ben Franklin's time because of its possibly devastating effects. Lightning
currents can rise to peak values of hundreds of kiloamperes in microsec-
onds. Average peak currents for clound-to-ground strokes are in the range
of tens of kiloamperes. Lightning traveling down conductors can cause serious damage. Furthermore, arcing potentials are severe because the inductance and resistance of conductors is not low enough to prevent extreme
voltage buildups at such high currents. Because of these current levels, good
grounding and routing practice (especially for lightning rods) is important.
Even underground cabling is not safe. Lightning can penetrate tens of feet
into the ground. In addition to direct effects, radiated lightning energy can
be readily coupled into power and signal wiring.

Lightning protection has traditionally included lightning rods (Franklin's invention), arcing voltage-suppression devices, nonlinear resistances
(thyristors), zener diode voltage-clipping devices, filters and transformers.
Usually, no simple technique is completely satisfactory; several methods are
commonly used in combination. One problem is that the high energy that
must be absorbed by a protection device may destroy it.

Power transients can be caused by many conditions in addition to lightning, including switching of loads and generating equipment by power companies or faults or other line problems in the distribution system (including

customer effects delivered to the lines). Transient supression devices similar to those intended to avoid the effects of lightning are effective methods of protection. The question of power quality is discussed in the next section.

The effects of static discharge have been known for centuries. The first written description was apparently by Thales (600 B.C.), who observed that amber rubbed with cloth took on unusual properties that could be attributed to charge. Basically, two dissimilar materials (such as those with differing dielectric constants) can, when in contact, transfer electrons from one to the other, resulting in trapped charge. Rubbing encourages this transfer. Everyone is familiar with the process of walking across a carpet on a dry day and touching a light switch or some other grounded device and receiving a shock. Voltage buildups in the vicinity of 15,000 V are not difficult to achieve. The shock is the result of the arc breakdown process by which the voltage differences are equalized. Static electricity is not ordinarily dangerous to humans because of the low current. However, sensitive electronic equipment used in contemporary computer and data-processing equipment can be severely damaged if not protected.

Most equipment manufacturers include protection against static discharge effects. The techniques used are generally zener diodes or similar low-power voltage-clamping devices. Sometimes users of sensitive equipment provide an environment that inhibits charge buildup. For example, humidity kept in the range of approximately 40 percent or above helps reduce static charge buildup. Conductive mats, carpets, component shields, and other materials need not be highly conductive of electricity to perform effectively. However, they must be conductive enough to prevent charge buildup under ordinary activity and handling. Antistatic sprays have been available for many years, advertised mostly to prevent "static-cling" of clothing. Similar products have been developed to protect computer rooms and electrical components. When sprayed on a carpet, they inhibit charge buildup for many hours. These techniques are in general less reliable than protective devices.

Information Disposal Devices

The disposal of printed or recorded data can create special problems if classified, private, proprietary, or sensitive data are not to be freely divulged. The security of computer data has been breached because computer printouts that were intended to be thrown away were intercepted and read. A secure installation should include equipment for destroying magnetic tape, disks, cartridges, microfilm, microfiche, printouts, and other materials.

All forms of information storage media can be destroyed by fire. However, burning requires special facilities and secure conveyance techniques.

In many situations, it is more economical to destroy the information and reuse the recording medium. Since magnetic information storage media can be repeatedly used over long lifetimes, device destruction would be a last resort. Magnetic information cleansing is known as "degaussing."

Shredders or disintegrators can be used to cut paper into strips or bits. They range from very light-duty office models to powerful units intended for computer installations. The cost of the computer devices range from about $2,000 to $30,000. The performance differences involve size of destroyed material, volume of information per unit time, and such accessories as automatic packaging of material and the ability to destroy bound or stapled documents without disassembly.

Typical shred sizes range from 1/4 to 1/32 of an inch. Disintegration involves cross-cutting action. Sizes of resulting pieces can range from about 1/2 inch by 1/32 inch to dust. Destruction rates range up to 1,500 lb/hr. Microfiche data can be shredded, but thermal destruction devices are generally preferable.

Degaussers generate magnetic fields that remove the magnetic domain alignment patterns that store information on tapes or disks. Degaussers can be used on standard or cartridge tape reels, disks, drums, floppy disks, cassettes, and magnetic cards. Unfortunately, because the required magnetic field strength (approximately 1,500 Oersteds) is not easy to impress on all of the volume to be erased without special design features, multiple degaussers are typically required for multiple media.

Partitioned Hardware

Contemporary high-technology systems raise a major issue for computer security in that hardware and software errors (or implanted overrides) can conceivably be used to interconnect users who should be separated. For example, users with security clearances working on classified data could be connected into the same multiplexer, port contender, or computer as uncleared users. All security-cleared users without common need to know could also be connected by the same channels as could users handling private, proprietary, or other sensitive information along with users who are not intended recipients of the data.

Such connections do not pose any problem as long as there is no hardware failure, no software failure, no surreptitious bypass in the hardware, and no surreptitious bypass in the software. For a variety of reasons, such error-free operation is difficult to guarantee. Hardware and software shared by users who must be separated pose significant problems.

To address this dilemma, researchers have begun to develop more secure systems. (See the description of kernelized software in chapter 6.)

Others have worked on hardware partitioning or kernelizing, in conjunction with the software approaches. Hardware or firmware methods are addressed in this section.

One of the most obvious ways to ensure separation is to use completely different equipment. For example, a computer used for classified processing can be restricted to users with security clearance as high as the highest classification level processed by the computer. Although this step might not guarantee need-to-know separation, it does minimize the risks. A single computer system can be used sequentially for one community of users followed by another with separation assurance if separate peripheral memory devices (such as tape or disk) are used. Normally, a combination of memory device-addressing restrictions or hard-wired switching or disconnect procedures are required.

Purging the residual central memory is also effective. In some cases, this method means rebooting the operating system or bringing up a new operating system. User controls (such as dial-up connections and passwords) must be converted from one configuration to the next.

Sometimes a particular piece of equipment can be configured in hardware so that for all practical purposes it behaves like separate pieces of equipment. For example, in port-contender partitioning, a ROM inserted in the device can be programmed to restrict certain classes of users or input lines to contend only for certain classes of port-output lines. In addition, hardware can be added to ensure that unintended connections result in no harm. For example lines or families of lines can be encrypted for processing data through an incompletely robust device. Users outside the encryption class would not find any possibilities beyond annoyance in the event of such a connection. Finally, personnel access, modifications, and repairs to such hardware should be carefully controlled.

Facilities Protection

Personnel control is fundamental to security, especially to computer security because of the high value of computer and information assets and because of the great potential for unauthorized personnel to cause damage. Physical and information assets must also be protected from fire, water, and heat. Locating critical facilities below grade or on the lower floors of multistory buildings is dangerous because of water drainage from plumbing, diverted rain, and flood.

Finally, despite all the protection devices available, a plan to respond to circumvention of any type should be prepared that will mitigate the effect of the occurrence.

Fire Protection Systems

Fire prevention, detection, and suppression are critically important to a computer-security program. Computing and data-processing equipment is generally extremely sensitive to heat, smoke, and water damage. Many peripheral devices are sensitive to particle contamination such as those caused by smoke. Most computer areas are replete with magnetic tapes and paper listings. Although magnetic tape does not burn well, the reels and closure bands are highly combustible, as is paper. Fumes created by the burning of such materials can be toxic. Heat and soot deposits can damage or destroy electronic and some mechanical components. To compound the situation, the most common, reliable, and effective means to fight fires is to use water, in the form of automatic fire-protection sprinkler systems. Although water can damage certain computer components and circuitry, especially if they are electrically active, automatic sprinkler systems have established a reputation for safety and reliability since their introduction in 1878. All sprinkler piping and heads are subjected to hydrostatic tests after they are installed. As a result, such systems are less likely to cause inadvertent water damage than ordinary water systems sometimes found in computer rooms.

Fire prevention is largely a question of human attentiveness to common rules and ordinary care, as well as conformance of facility design and construction to the electrical and construction codes. Government agencies, insurance companies, and the National Fire Protection Association (NFPA 75) specify more restrictive standards for electronic computer facilities. Noncombustible materials and finishes should be used whenever possible. A continuing program to limit the presence of fuel and such flammable materials as manuals, printouts, magnetic tapes, disk covers, and cleaning fluids is essential to maintaining a fire-safe environment.

Because many companies depend heavily on a central computer center for payroll, supplier payments, accounting, and other records, fire damage could be a devastating blow to the company's business health. As a result, there is considerable motivation to minimize the effect of any fires that may occur by early detection, suppression without damage to equipment or personnel, and the prevention of spreading.

Three basic types of fire-detection systems are commonly used in computer facilities: ionization, light scattering, and heat detection. Ionization smoke-detection devices are probably the most popular. They use a small amount of radioactive material that ionizes the air molecules in a sensing chamber. This ionization in turn creates conductivity, allowing current to flow between two charged electrodes in the chamber. Heavy smoke particles reduce this conductivity by attaching to ions, which decreases their mobility and consequently limits the amount of current. When current is reduced to a specified threshold, it sets off a smoke-detection signal or alarm. Ionization detectors are sensitive to very small invisible particles from open flames.

Light-scattering smoke detectors depend basically on the light-scattering properties of smoke particles in the air within the detector. Smoke particles scatter the light emitted from a lamp within the detector onto a photoelectric device. Light-scattering detectors are most sensitive to visible smoke from smoldering or slow burning fires. Heat-detection devices are generally based on bimetal strips, diaphragm-vented chamber covers, leaf springs retained by eutectic metal, thermocouples, or thermopiles. Smoke detectors are more commonly used than heat detectors in computer facilities because of their higher sensitivity, enabling them to detect a fire earlier.

Once fire is detected, a variety of responses are possible, from room flooding with a fire extinguishant, light or sound alarms, to hand extinguishers. Hand fire extinguishers can be used if the fire is small enough to be controlled by computer room personnel. The most common types use water, CO_2, dry chemicals, and Halon 1211. Water is very effective on wood, paper, and plastics, but should not be sprayed on energized electrical equipment because of the potential hazards of shock and equipment damage. Dry chemicals create a cleanup problem, so they should not be located within the computer room. CO_2 extinguishers are suitable for fires involving an electric shock hazard but are not very effective in extinguishing paper and plastic fires. Halon 1211 hand-held extinguishers are generally satisfactory, though somewhat more expensive, and are rated for electrical as well as wood, paper, and plastic fires. Halon 1211 is easy to clean up and extinguishes fire rapidly. However, such extinguishers should not be used in poorly ventilated or confined spaces because they can lead to toxicity and suffocation.

Every computer facility should designate an emergency team which has been trained to respond to fire by ringing fire alarms; evacuating the building; using hand fire extinguishers, when safe; assisting and advising the fire department; shutting down computer equipment and removing power as required; checking sprinkler system valves; protecting computer cabinets from water and smoke with plastic sheets or tarps; and manually activating fire-suppression systems.

Automatic fire-suppression equipment is an essential part of major or critical computer areas. Smoke or heat detectors can automatically trigger the systems. More commonly, some form of logic is incorporated so that a false alarm or failure of a single detector will trigger an alarm but that two or more detectors actuate the suppression system. More sophisticated logic is sometimes used.

Automatic fire suppression is needed for those cases where staff using hand fire extinguishers are driven out of the building by toxic gases or smoke or when the building is unoccupied. The fire department may take many minutes to respond; if the fire becomes well developed, the fire department might need to use heavy water hose streams to control the fire. Automatic suppression systems will begin to control a fire until the fire department arrives, resulting in less damage. Water, Halon, or both are used in suppresion systems. CO_2 is also a choice but introduces personnel hazards such as suffocation and severely reduced visibility. Water systems can be supplemented by extinguishers for early response to reduce or eliminate water on computer components. However, it is much easier to repair water damage than to rebuild a facility. Personnel can prevent or minimize water damage by covering sensitive equipment with plastic sheets if there is time before evacuation.

The use of Halon in fire suppression systems is an effective (though expensive and less reliable) choice. Halon is a halogenated hydrocarbon (hydrogen atoms are replaced by atoms from the halogen series) that functions as a flame-extinguishing agent. Halon is relatively harmless (at carefully designed gas-air ratios) to personnel and equipment. It is generally used in one of two forms: bromotrifluoremethane ($CBrF_3$) or bromochlorodifluoromethane ($CBrClF_2$). The former is identified as Halon 1301 and is generally used for automatic total flooding systems in the United States because it is less toxic. Because Halon 1301 is discharged as a gas at concentrations well below those necessary to suffocate the fire, the principle extinguishing method is chemical inhibition of the combustion process within the flame. The hot char layer on the fuel is not quenched (as with water) and must be air-cooled below the reignition temperature of the combustible vapors evolved from the solid fuel. Therefore, it is essential that all doors, duct openings, floor drains, and other air sources be sealed to prevent the heavy Halon gas/air mixture from escaping from the fire area before the fire is extinguished. Gaseous systems must be designed by competent firms in strict accordance with NFPA standards. Nitrogen is usually used in Halon 1301 systems to increase pressure, which in turn, reduces the time to discharge the Halon. Halon 1301 is highly volatile.

The other Halon form is Halon 1211, or BCF, which is generally used only in handheld extinguishers in computer rooms. Halon gases are relatively low in toxicity, noncorrosive, nonconductive, and discharge at only slightly below freezing. They reduce visibility only slightly and have excellent penetration and flame-extinguishing properties. Halon 1211 is discharged as a gas-liquid mixture and works by cooling, smothering, and chemical interference with the combustion process. Its deleterious effects on plastics and elastometers are higher than for Halon 1301.

Halon gases may cause toxic effects in humans at percent-by-volume levels in the vicinity of those required to extinguish most fires. Halon 1301 is not harmful for short exposures up to about 15 percent-by-volume concentrations. Halon 1211 is safe only up to about 5 percent. Most fires require concentration in the 5 percent range, although some deep-seated hot spots may require higher concentrations.

Halon gases are generally most effective against Class B (flammable liquid and vapor) and Class C (electrical) fires. Class A (wood, paper, plastic, cloth) fires are more difficult to control because of the inherent propensity to develop deep-seated fires. Early fire detection and rapid discharge are essential requirements of Halon systems.

Halon, at less than adequate gas-air extinguishing concentrations, can react with fire to produce halogen acids (hydrogen bromide, hydrogen fluoride, free bromide, and—in the case of BCF—hydrogen chloride and chlorine). These acids can be harmful or lethal to humans if inhaled in significant quantities. They are detectable by smell. Other disadvantages of Halon systems are cost and system reliability (typically significantly lower than for automatic water sprinkler systems). However Halon 1301 is an attractive choice for the total flooding of fires in major computer centers because it acts quickly to extinguish surface fires with little damage or cleanup. Several companies market Halon systems.

Compartmentalizing the fire will discourage spreading. Floor-to-ceiling insulating walls (fire walls), fire dampers in ducts, fixed fire windows (or no windows), and normally closed or automatically closing fire doors can be built in to seal off the most expensive and programatically critical equipment, such as the computer mainframe or large central memory units, from the rest of the computer room. Halon 1301 total flooding could then be used to protect inside the compartment, into which no tapes, reels, plastic disk covers, maintenance manuals, or other combustibles would be introduced. The rest of the computer facility could be protected by automatic water sprinkler systems, which are more reliable and effective.

Finally, protective devices alone do not eliminate the possibility of circumvention of some type. Electrical supervision of critical system valves and other components, periodic inspection, and system testing are required. Computer security staff should consider developing a plan to mitigate the effects of fires.

Power Conditioning

Manufacturers of data-processing equipment usually warn that equipment performance depends on the quality of the power. Although utility companies attempt to provide consistent power, a number of problems affect the robustness of the computing environment.

Short-term irregularities. These "glitches" are microsecond or millisecond deviations from the expected sinusoidal waveform. The relatively high-frequency content of the energy threatens logic circuits. Glitches usually occur when energy is coupled onto power lines by lightning or heavy machinery power switching in the vicinity, but may be the result of equipment switching by the utility.

Sags and surges (long-term irregularities). These deviations in supply occur over cycles instead of fractions of a cycle. They are often caused by high-current events like lightning or major equipment switching, especially at the utility plant.

Overvoltage/undervoltage. The voltage requirement specifications for most computer systems are in the ±10 percent range. Power companies usually cannot guarantee this quality over their entire service area. One of the major factors is distance away from the generating source, which makes voltage more load-dependent. Another is the somewhat unpredictable variation in loads created by consumers. Undervoltage or brownout also sometimes occurs when the utility company cannot furnish as much power as consumers are trying to use because of unexpected loads, generating equipment failure, or maintenance. Both overvoltage and undervoltage can cause various components to overheat. Motors are probably the most seriously affected, and these may be part of the computer facility power-generation process.

Outage (blackout). During a complete power failure, it might be impossible to execute a graceful computer shutdown. An orderly shutdown can frequently save a considerable amount of recovery processing.

Common-mode noise. Common-mode effects appear on the high and low side of the power line. They can be caused by fault currents or lightning, especially when grounding is imperfect.

The major computer-security concerns involve saving data during a shutdown, protecting the integrity of the equipment, preventing anomalous behavior (soft errors) in the data processing, and providing for personnel safety (such as assuring emergency lighting).

Power-line monitors are often used to assess the power quality at a computer site. These widely available devices can be used to quantify and categorize the problems that occur over time. Recorded values are available through visual displays or printouts. Power quality problems can be mitigated or solved with filters, isolation transformers, regulators, power line conditioners, and auxiliary power sources (UPS, IPS, backup power), fuses, and circuit breakers. Filters are generally the least expensive and also the least satisfying method. Although filters can be used to remove some glitch energy, the typical high current of utility power, and their insertion loss make filters of minimal value.

Isolation transformers remove common-mode noise and may be used in some cases to adjust voltage. They also prevent data signals from being coupled outside a secure area on power lines. However, their use should be cost-justified. (An autotransformer is not an isolation transformer. These devices use common windings and provide no isolation.) Regulators can be used to control voltage fluctuations within limits. The selection of regulators depends on whether there are other problems than fluctuating voltage levels. Power-line conditioners usually combine regulation and filtering.

Auxiliary power sources can include diesel motor-generator sets or battery-driven power generators or both. The most widely used technique is the uninterruptible power system (UPS). UPS equipment is available from a number of manufacturers and systems, and can be selected with a variety of features and capabilities. Basically, a UPS uses one of two sources of input power (utility or battery) to generate output power. If the utility power is interrupted, battery power is used to drive an inverter or similar device to generate AC power. The UPS might be required only for minutes or a portion of an hour while the computer system is brought to a controlled halt. Alternatively, a motor generator might be brought up so that computer power can continue indefinitely.

Less-powerful systems include interruptible power systems (IPS), which are useful only for systems that do not depend on volatile memory and systems that provide "ridethrough" of power loss for a fraction of a second.

Environmental Control

Large computer systems require environmental control. Extreme variations in temperature can affect electronic circuitry, tapes, disks, and drums. Low humidity can lead to static electricity. Raised floors are often built in computer rooms to facilitate environmental control. Air-conditioning systems control temperatures and air moisture; they are generally set at 72 °F and about 45 percent humidity. Air-conditioning units are a computer-security concern because the loss of the air conditioning could mean the loss of the computer. Therefore, many of the same considerations that apply to computers (particularly physical protection, backup, recovery) apply to air conditioning.

Water Detection

Water can cause extensive damage to computer systems and associated hardware, including electrical shorts, physical deterioration, soft data errors, safety hazards, and deposits that must be cleaned up. Because the presence of small amounts of moisture are readily detectable by sensing devices, extensive damage can possibly be avoided by early identification (for example, Water Alert® monitors manufactured by Dorlen Products in Milwaukee). Sensing devices can be strategically placed so that a minor leak will be identified and fixed before it becomes a major problem. Sensors can be battery-operated or connected to an AC power source. They can operate independently or connected to a master alarm system. Because sensors are not expensive (a basic model costs less than $100), they are often an effective preventive measure.

Backup, Recovery, and Service Centers

A company that suffers a major disaster affecting its computing capability has several options. It can simply stop computing until its equipment or power can be restored. However, very few companies of any size can afford this option. Not only do businesses depend heavily on computers, but the recovery from a major disaster could take uncomfortably long. A widely quoted statistic for 1981 major computer disasters shows an average of three months was required to restore full computer operation.

Some companies are fortunate enough to have distributed computing capability, or at least dual sites, which provide backup. Satellite networks and other wide-area data-communication networks enhance this type of backup. Many companies with similar facilities agree to provide backup to each other in an emergency—an attractive and inexpensive approach. However, there is always some uncertainty regarding how freely one company might let another company use its facilities if the host company's operations were being adversely affected. In any event, companies with mutual backup agreements should periodically test compatibility by running critical applications (preferably using backup tapes and disks) on each other's systems.

Many companies offer a wide variety of backup and recovery services. These services include full-service bureaus that perform computing for a company during the recovery period; "hot sites" with computers that are intended to be turned over for operation by the recovering company; empty "shell sites" configured for computer installations; prefabricated computer-site construction services; and computer facility preparation services that will provide a data-processing center in space provided by the afflicted company.

Service bureaus are generally an expensive alternative and are usually limited in processing volume or capabilities. Their advantage is that no expenditures are necessary unless a disaster occurs. There are several service centers in various parts of the country. At least eleven companies provide hot sites, some with multiple locations in various parts of the United States. Sizes range from 2,500 sq ft for the Arbat Systems Ltd DEC PDP-11 site to almost 100,000 sq ft at the Sun Information Services Co. Sungard Philadelphia site. Usually, companies pay a monthly membership fee (typically $300 to $5,500 per month) plus a usage fee if service becomes necessary. Membership limits run from about 10 to 100. Most companies limit the usage period to a maximum time ranging from 6 weeks to 90 days. Hot sites typically offer particular types of computers with disk and tape memory support, fire detection and protection systems, data communications services and lines, power, air conditioning, and security (guards, alarms, closed circuit TV, and access control). Some well-known full-service bureaus are Comdisco Disaster Recovery Services, Inc.; Litton Systems, Inc., Mellonics Information Center; and Remote Computing Corporation.

Most hot sites also provide shell space. At least eight companies provide shell sites as their main service. The shell size ranges from about 1,000 sq ft to over 30,000 sq ft. Fees range from about $150 per month to about $1,500 per month (with increased use fees if the shell is utilized for a facility). Membership limitations range from about 15 to 100 and maximum use periods range from about 6 to 12 months. Some of the major companies providing shell site services are Data Processing Security, Inc.; Data Shield, Inc.; Eloigne Corp.; Emergency Computer Center, Inc.; and Wright Line Inc./Iron Mountain Group (Data Site).

Physical Protection

Facilities can also be protected with robust construction practices, such as building without windows; using fire walls; using safety valves to relieve water, steam, or gas pressure; not using water tanks or flat roof construction immediately above computers; and earthquake-resistant construction. Another common physical restraint is a security fence or similar barrier.

Surveillance and Intrusion Detection

Various surveillance methods can be used to ensure computer security, such as locks and security guard forces. More technological techniques include closed-circuit TV, sometimes with sophisticated enhancements such as control systems for sequencing multiple cameras on one or more displays; recording data, time, and location data on videotape; motion-alert processing; time-lapse recording; screen splitters; low light-level cameras; and tilt, pan and zoom features.

Ultrasonic, and microwave, or infrared intrusion alarms; and door/window switch alarms can be used to secure unattended computer facilities. Data from a network of alarms can be processed to help determine an appropriate response to a large-scale emergency.

Technical Control Centers

Many security functions can be consolidated in technical control centers (TCCs), such as remote diagnostics that speed troubleshooting and repair, security switching and disconnecting, and security monitoring. The consolidation of these functions and the centralization of communication equipment (modems, multiplexers, port contenders) into a center or centers is a powerful deterrent to interruption of services. Remote diagnostics are the most cost-effective service offerred by a TCC. Diagnostic testing can be performed over the entire communications link, which isolates problems and speeds restoration of services.

The maintenance of data security for communication paths passing through the TCC depends on several important principles:

1. Operating personnel who may be exposed to data must be carefully screened and cleared.
2. Physical separation of lines carrying different classes of data helps to reduce or eliminate coupling effects.
3. Tight physical security is necessary to prevent unauthorized equipment modification, information compromise, or vandalism.
4. Procedures and equipment must be carefully designed to prevent accidental misconnection or other forms of compromise.

TCCs are useful in monitoring the security of transactions taking place on the computing network. Monitoring can be controlled manually or automatically, and recording is an attractive option.

6 Protective Software Technology

Software plays an important role in computer security. The various categories of computer security software include access controls, encryption routines, kernelized or partitioned systems, risk analysis packages, comparators, and logging and auditing software.

Access Control Software

Many computer operating systems are so strongly oriented toward providing operational features that they provide relatively low-level security protection. In those applications where security concerns are important, some form of augmentation is often necessary.

It is always possible to build security into each application as part of its design. This approach has the advantage of providing security features that are tailored specifically to the application requirements. Its disadvantage is that many security features are usually duplicated on multiple applications.

The operating system can also be modified to provide the desired system security. Such modifications might be appropriate in a static operating system; however, contemporary operating systems are dynamic and evolving, requiring constant updates and new releases. In such environments, the operating system should remain under the control of the manufacturer for reliable maintenance, troubleshooting, and updates.

As a result, security augmentation packages have been developed by many companies that offer access control features. Several attributes should be considered in evaluating these packages:

1. The most effective packages are, as nearly as possible, transparent to the user. They must create minimal overhead and minimal interference with a user's normal routines.
2. Security packages are not universally applicable. Each is designed to interface with a particular operating system or a small number of variations. Most commercial security packages are designed to operate on IBM computers.
3. Such modifications as adding user authorizations and changing pass-

words should be done while the system is on-line. It is inefficient to bring the system down for these activities.

4. Unique individual access passwords are an important feature. One-way encryption for password storage is useful.
5. Logging of activities for examination for security or audit personnel is useful.
6. The system should disconnect or disable users or terminals after a prescribed number of incorrect access attempts. Constant or increasing time delays can be equally effective.
7. File-access controls can be implemented using file passwords, user-access tables (users certified for particular file-access and control privileges), or file-access tables (containing information that maps files to user privileges).
8. Message generation for users, operators, or security personnel is a useful attribute.
9. The control of connect time and screen display time while the terminal is inactive is useful to prevent compromise if a user leaves an active terminal unattended.
10. Default assignment ensures that no parameters are left unassigned, which could create unexpected vulnerabilities.
11. Integrity protection controlling write privilege can deter the intentional or accidental overwriting of important data.
12. Backup and recovery features can be of special interest for critical data and processes.
13. Terminal identification is a useful parameter.
14. The automatic enforcement of periodic password changes (deletion after specified time intervals) is often desirable.
15. Discrimination between dial-up lines and hardwired lines in the enforced security features is an attribute.
16. Time-of-day restrictions for particular users or terminals gives additional security flexibility.
17. Ease of installation and maintenance; vendor support, simplicity of training and operation; and reasonable cost are other important features.

Many security packages now include most or all these attributes. They range from about $10,000 to $50,000, with leasing a frequent option. The best-known packages include ACF2 (Cambridge Systems Group); RACF (IBM); Top Secret ™ (CGA Software Products Group); SECURE ™ (Boole and Babbage); SAC ™ (Electronic Data Systems); Guardian (On-Time Software International); and SURVEILLANCE (Tower Systems, Inc.). Some special data management systems provide additional capabilities, such as ASM2 (Cambridge Systems Group) and TD-FAST/VSE (Tower Systems, Inc.).

The listed attributes are not always sufficient criteria to select an appropriate package. To judge the selectivity of a security software package, it may be necessary to use it in an evolving environment. Some companies make this easier by offering controlled flexibility in their security features and by offering lease options. In these cases, a package can be leased for a trial period and the security features can be implemented gradually. Users can then assess the cost-effectiveness of the product and the degree of control necessary in their environment.

Encryption Software

Software encryption involves a variety of techniques, similar to the methods used for hardware encryption. In fact, the most popular hardware encryption techniques (DES and public-key encryption) are available in software routines. However, DES was designed specifically for hardware implementation, and it is less efficient when implemented in software. Many other public domain encryption schemes are used; others are proprietary company products.

However, there are some subtle differences in choosing between hardware and software encryption. For example, passwords are almost always generated, processed, stored, and retrieved by software. Software encryption is therefore more natural for passwords. The most common reasons for encrypting passwords are preventing the exposure of clear-text passwords if anyone accidentally or intentionally gains access to the password file. In addition, where passwords are generated in one process and loaded into a computer file in a different process, the generation of encrypted passwords prevents operations or password control personnel from being exposed to clear-text passwords. Finally, remote terminals that communicate with computers use communications links (usually phone lines) that are less secure than the host computer. If the passwords used on these terminals are transmitted in encrypted form they are less vulnerable to tapping or other interception.

However, encrypted passwords are of no value if they can be used in the same way as clear-text passwords or can be used to obtain clear-text passwords. To reduce or eliminate this potential problem, one-way encryption is often used for passwords; that is, the clear-text password cannot be recovered using a knowledge of the encrypted password. This method is obviously the opposite of the motivation in communication where recovery of the clear-text by the intended recipient is required. In addition, the encrypted version is not useful for entry into the computer system because entries to the system are passed through a one-way encryption process before they are compared with the encrypted password table. Although DES is not intended to be a one-way encryption process, it can be modified to make it one-way. Many other encryption techniques are designed as one-way systems.

Software encryption for file storage is also a natural application. The portability of tapes, disks, cartridges, and similar devices makes data theft a potential concern. The encryption of such data lessens its vulnerability. Several commercial software encryption codes are available, such as DEF ™ , a DES based code from Applied Software, Inc.

Comparators

Software should not be changed without authorization and accountability. The changes made should be controlled and should not go beyond those authorized. Software comparators provide one way to achieve the necessary control. A comparator is a computer code comparison routine that details the differences between old and new versions of the code. An example of a commercial comparator package is RES-Q ™ (Quality Systems). This package, and others, do a line-by-line comparison of source code and detail and report differences. The technique is also useful for comparing files, reports, dumps, and other data and programs. Comparators are a useful tool for EDP auditors and production control personnel.

Audit Software

Audit packages provide information appropriate for audit examination. Although most of the access-control security packages mentioned previously provide audit-trail information, audit software packages include special features. Generally, the most interesting and useful features are commands that control the sampling, reporting and displaying of data independently from users and the system development group. Security protection for the package is also important to prevent interference, monitoring, or spoofing. The evaluation of audit packages involves not only the capabilities of the product, but also its compatibility with a specific computer and operating system.

Kernelized Systems

As long as all users of a computer system have the same privileges and needs for access to information, computer access is the main security issue. However, usually usage is considerably different for different users. For example, some users may have classified access and some may not, levels of classification may be different, "need-to-know" privileges may be different, and all users may not need access to private information, to name only a few reasons.

In such cases, the issue is preventing users from getting information to which they have no right. Most computer professionals concede that skilled systems programmers can find ways to access most information in computer systems with which they are familiar. Because of this vulnerability, special steps must be taken to prevent unauthorized access to information in some computer systems.

There are two basic ways to approach segmentation of computer systems: hardware kernelization and software kernelization. Software kernelization depends on operating system checks to ensure that particular users access only the portions of the memory to which they have a right and perform no unauthorized accesses or transfers. This task is not difficult conceptually, but secure implementation can be a problem.

A kernelized software system has several requirements:

1. It must always be invoked.
2. It must be impossible to bypass it, override it, or change it.
3. Every possible operational situation must be able to be tested and analyzed so that the kernel performance can be completely ensured and certified. Certification has proved to be an elusive goal for all practical systems.

Development of kernelized software began at least in the late 1960s, when Honeywell, MIT, GE and others worked on the Multics, Multics-Aim and Guardian systems. Ford Aerospace and Honeywell worked on PSOS and KSOS during the 1970s; recently, Honeywell has devoted considerable effort to SCOMP, a combined hardware/software kernelized system. Major kernelized security efforts are also under way at Control Data Corporation and Digital Equipment Corporation.

The general multilevel security (MLS) problem has been of special concern to the Department of Defense, which has defined eight types of systems:

D—minimal

C1—discretionary

C2—controlled access

B1—labeled

B2—structured

B3—security domains

A1—verified design

A2—verified implementation

No computers have yet been assigned A ratings by the Defense Department, although SCOMP is apparently a serious contender for the A1 category.

Some kernelized systems are based on a reference monitor, which controls the flow of information within protected computer systems, between subjects such as processes or users, and objects or information units. The security policy enforced by a reference monitor is generally in accordance with a Department of Defense-suggested mathematical model. A basic tenet of the policy is that reading data having a higher classification level than the reading process is not allowed, nor is writing down from a process at a higher level than the receiving object. The former condition is sometimes called the "simple security" property and the latter is called the "security*-property."

The SCOMP implementation combines kernelized software and hardware implemented on a Honeywell Level 6 minicomputer. The Level 6 is a bus-structured 16-bit minicomputer. An intensive effort was made in the SCOMP program to increase operational efficiency, since low efficiency was a major disadvantage in the early kernelized systems. SCOMP will also be available in a Tempest-protected version.

Risk Analysis

Risk analysis is a formal technique for assessing the expected cost of a vulnerability (for example, annual loss expectancy dollars) and the cost or amortized cost of installing a safeguard to reduce or eliminate the vulnerability. The significant security weaknesses include, for example, those that result in financial loss, loss of protected information, and loss of a function that is a critical link with other parts of the organization.

Most vulnerabilities can be quantified at least roughly. Financial loss is the most obvious. There are some less-quantifiable forms of financial loss, however. Loss of information could prove embarrassing to the company. Embarrassment cannot be easily quantified. If the loss of information and resulting embarrassment are influential in reducing financial support for the company, for example, the loss becomes quantitative. Such a situation might also result in lawsuits against the company. Part of the risk analysis might be to identify a confidence level or some other accuracy measure along with the risk assessment.

Critical information or processing capability is usually viewed as being a crucial link in a chain if it is badly needed elsewhere. For example, scientific data gathered during the Mount St. Helens eruption was critical to scientists studying volcanic activity. The data had to be protected against loss during the analyses. Loss of the data would have been a serious impediment to analytical activities because the data could not be duplicated by retesting. Quantifying such losses of irreplaceable data is extremely difficult. However, some estimates are possible. For example, if a university thrives financially because of its research status, its level of financial support might be dependent upon the outcome of analytical programs that receive wide public attention. It might also have bearing in a battle between companies to win lucrative research contracts or grants. It is important that the confidence level of the estimates be consistent throughout the analysis so that decisions can be made with relative confidence that the assumptions were reasonably sound.

Most safeguards installed to reduce or eliminate financial risk can be costed out directly or amortized over a number of years. As a result, the comparison between costs and benefits is as realistic as possible. However, decisions are not bound to follow the results of a risk analysis. First, the results may be only rough estimates because the assumptions were uncertain. Second, there may be pressures on the decisionmakers that could not be quantified by the risk-analysis process. Obviously human judgment is the final authority, but risk analysis can give surprisingly accurate guidance in making many decisions.

The main basis for risk analysis lies in quantifying potential loss and the cost of safeguards to prevent the loss. The expected value of the loss is:

$$E = IP_L$$

where I is the potential loss and P_L is the probability of the occurrence of the loss. To make the results more applicable, an annual loss expectancy is calculated:

$$ALE = IF$$

where F is the probability that the loss will occur in a year.

The use of risk analysis is further facilitated by a quantifying technique first suggested by Robert Courtney (then with IBM) in 1977 and later adopted as a federal guideline in *FIPS PUB65* (Federal Information Processing Standards Publication). The technique depends on logarithmic increments; therefore a value f is assigned to be related to the base 10 logarithm of F. One way to do this is to assign f based on a table:

Frequency	Value of f
Once in 300 years	1
Once in 30 years	2
Once in 3 years	3
Once in 100 days	4
Once in 10 days	5
Once in 1 day	6

.

.

.

where

$$\dot{F} = \frac{10^{f-3}}{3}.$$

The estimated loss can be handled similarly:

Estimated loss	Value of i
10	1
100	2
1,000	3
10,000	4
100,000	5
1,000,000	6

.

.

.

where

$$\text{ALE} = \frac{10^{f+i-3}}{3}$$

For example, if a devastating fire could be expected to occur once in 30 years, and equipment worth $1 million would be lost, the *ALE* computation is:

$$ALE = \frac{10^{2 + 6 - 3}}{3} \approx \$30,000$$

When the risk of loss is understood, it is easier to determine the appropriate expenditure for protective measures. To be comprehensive, this process must be invoked for each major cost item. Once the appropriate safeguards have been selected, it is understood that there are still loss possibilities, but the loss expectancy should be acceptable. The level of risk is even more difficult to assess for the entire program than for individual vulnerabilities. If all the threats were independent and none involved intentional attacks, the solution would be simply the probability calculation for independent events:

$$P_L = 1 - (1 - p_a)(1 - p_b)(1 - p_c) \ldots$$

$$= 1 - \prod_n (1 - p_i)$$

where P_L is the overall probability of loss and p_i represents the independent loss probabilities. Introducing dependencies makes the problem more complex; introducing the thinking processes of people that might intentionally attack the system makes the situation untractable. Even despite its incomplete ability to analyze, its limited accuracy, and its other shortcomings, risk analysis is an indispensible tool for guidance.

Several consulting companies specialize in risk analysis; a few software packages have been developed to aid users in performing risk analysis. The best known software system is Panrisk ™ from Pansophic Systems, Inc. These software packages systematize the approach for the user. Data must be furnished for a particular system and cost estimates must be made to the best degree of accuracy the user can provide. The risk-analysis package implements the appropriate computations.

Risk analysis packages also provide a format or methodology for gathering data. Knowing what questions to ask in a risk analysis is a valuable part of the exercise. Finally, the results of risk analysis computations are displayed in tabular form that can be interpreted easily. This feature is especially valuable since the final decisions on how to act on risk analysis results is highly subjective. An effective display of the results can help to ensure the most judicious decisions.

The advantages of using consulting organizations for risk analysis include their expertise and experience, the crosscheck of an independent view, and training for the utilizing organization in their methodology. Consulting firms also provide the opportunity to spend financial resources instead of personnel resources in cases where money is available and personnel on the payroll are already busy and closely matched to the business activity.

Banking Backup Software

One of the most serious operational problems that a bank experiences when computing capability is lost is inability to process checks. Various software routines are available. Viable Information Processing Systems (Survival Check System) has developed a backup program that addresses this problem.

Such systems allow a bank to process checks on another bank's computers during emergencies. The software is portable; modification and recompiling are obviated. The Survival Check System is based on IBM 3890 implementation. However, because the system is simplified to include only critical functions, it addresses only a limited number of the many problems that occur during computer loss.

7

Evaluating Security Technology

In addition to surveying the constituents of computer security and protective measures, methods for evaluating the success of computer-security programs must also be reviewed. This process is somewhat analogous to a quality-assurance program in manufacturing, where after-the-fact measurements are made to evaluate product quality.

Basically, security evaluations require identifying measurable events so that relative strengths and weaknesses in a program can be assessed quantitatively. These data, although sometimes difficult to generate, can be powerful indicators of where computer-security techniques have been overapplied, underapplied, or applied to an ideal degree.

EDP Auditing

One of the most accepted and widely used techniques for assessing a computer-security program is to secure or hire an independent organization trained in data-processing auditing. Outside audits offer several advantages: independent assessments frequently reveal shortcomings overlooked by the day-to-day operators of the program; and computer-security personnel may not have the same degree of insight and training that skilled EDP auditors can apply to an in-depth probe of the security program.

Effective auditing depends largely on the availability of a comprehensive amount of auditable data and an audit trail. The audit trail must record incidents so that the auditor can determine the sequence of events after the fact. Audits should be frequent, random, independent, and visible. Visibility, in particular, is a deterrent to deliberate security violations. Many events can provide auditable data, including the "day file" of computer log-ons and file-access data; documentation on the details of the security software used; applications programs; system operating instructions; and system runstreams.

Some threats, such as sequential password guesses, are relatively easy to detect in an audit. Others, such as exploiting design anomalies or errors, are extremely difficult. In either case, it is important to protect the data-gathering process to reach a correct conclusion. Also, the audit function should not accidentally or intentionally excerpt protected information. Neither is a trivial problem, and both have been extensively discussed in the literature.

There are several widely used EDP audit procedures. For example, review of the computer center should include risk analysis, physical plant review, and a review of procedures and operating methods (access control, handling and distribution of output, scheduling, and information destruction). Review of security software and hardware might incorporate a number of tests of computer-access controls; file or database access controls; detection, records, and follow-up of security violations; and control of data storage and movement (clearing memory, protecting tape labels, and restricting destination of sensitive data).

An audit of applications systems (systems selected by risk analysis) should cover both the development phase (life-cycle events, acceptance and control responsibility, control guidelines, and post-implementation reviews), as well as the operation phase (develop and apply various audit tools to determine the effectiveness of controls within and operational integrity of an application system). Finally, an audit should review disaster-recovery preparations for facilities, software, and data.

Many of these procedures have been discussed in previous sections. An effective EDP audit program comprehensively covers all security considerations, just as an implementation program should. However, several tools and techniques are unique to an audit program. Area selection is a computerized technique to help the auditor select locations from among multiorganization structures. The intent is to optimize audit resources by evaluating key indicators, such as financial or control information.

Scoring is a planning technique for the systematic selection of computer application systems for audit. It uses quantifiable characteristics that are significant as assessed by risk analysis.

Multisite audit software is useful when regional or other peripheral computing centers are served by a central system development and programming staff. A set of audit programs can be developed to test computer applications run at multiple locations. Multisite audit software is usually more cost-effective than custom audit packages for each site.

A competency center is a centralized computer system that runs audit software programs. This technique is especially useful within multilocation organizations. Parallel operation can be used to check new or recently modified application programs by comparing production data and files with both former and new procedures to identify any differences for analysis. An integrated test facility is used in testing large computer-application systems when it is not practical to use separate test data. Internal auditors' test data are used to review the functions of an application that are internal to the computer.

Standard data-entry procedures involve entering a standard input into an application program and verifying the expected results. The technique is limited, but it can reveal unexpected changes in the execution of applications programs, due to software or hardware changes.

While the objective of standard data entry is to check computer performance, computer simulation is intended to test data. That is, data normally used in an application are processed using a simplified program intended to duplicate only the essential processes. This technique has the advantage of checking a potentially large number of procedures involved in conveying data to the computer.

Transaction-selection audit techniques use a special computer program to select transactions for review based on certain probabilities. Statistical sampling procedures can be used, estimates of measurable parameters (such as volume, connect time, or errors) can be made, and items exceeding some predefined thresholds (such as numerous incorrect access attempts) can be flagged.

Audit functions can also be built into or embedded in applications programs to record data continuously for later analysis. Such techniques are more efficient when incorporated into the application program during development than retrofit functions.

Another longstanding audit practice traces the sequence of events followed during interdependent or linked transactions to examine and attempt to understand the complete sequence. Cost-accounting records are almost always maintained to provide equitable chargeback allocations of computing costs. These records typically show connect time, CPU time, or resources used. These data also provide valuable auditing information.

When it is difficult to reconstruct the logic operations of a computer during the EDP audit, the snapshot technique can prove helpful. This technique uses data records on portions of memory involved in a decision-making process, with the data records available at the time of interest. A preprogrammed triggering mechanism is added to print the results.

Mapping is done by a software tool that tracks whether individual program statements have been executed. This technique is useful during testing because it indicates program logic that has not been tested.

Flowcharting is a technique for displaying the interrelation of control features. Flowcharting helps to assess controls quickly and evaluate the overall impact of changes. An audit guide is a documentation of questions, follow-up actions, and steps to perform in carrying out an audit. Finally, the postinstallation audit is an evaluation technique for auditing application systems after they have been put into production. It involves a systematic evaluation of the actual operational effectiveness of control measures.

File and Transaction Monitoring

One of the most difficult tasks in a computer-security program is to prevent an authorized user of a computer system from using it in an unauthorized way. For example, a user must have relatively free access to a computer if the computer is to be an effective on-the-job tool. However, short of looking over the user's shoulder at all times, it is impossible to prevent use of the system for playing games and other, inappropriate personal business.

Although the level of such activities depends largely on the user's personal integrity, users can be motivated to exhibit more integrity if they know their activities may be observed. File and transaction monitoring are usually effective measures and also provide data to judge the degree of computer misuse.

On a computer system containing tens of thousands of files, it is not practical to examine each file. However, dumping and reading a small percentage (1 to 5 percent) is not only feasible, it is statistically significant. That is, the percentage of misuse found in a 1 to 5 percent sample would not be expected to differ significantly from the total percentage of misuse.

In addition to the statistical benefits, file monitoring deters misuse. There is no harm in publicizing the activity so that users are aware any misuse may be discovered. Although someone bent on improper activity could make it very difficult to detect, file monitoring does make such activities more difficult.

A variation on file monitoring is to flag a file in a random sample and request an assessment from the owner's supervisor. This procedure has the benefit of shifting some responsibility for monitoring a user's integrity to the user's supervisor, where it probably more properly belongs. Feedback and spot checks should be required, however, both to ensure that the supervisor does not neglect the task and to accumulate statistics for computer-security assessement. Transaction monitoring offers an additional benefit because records of computer activity need not be left in files. This requires that transaction-recording equipment be installed. The desirability of such an activity must be evaluated for each program.

Log Examination

Many activities on major computer systems are recorded in a system log file controlled by the operating system. This log provides such records and data as accountability, so that computer charges can be compiled; transaction records; audit-trail data; and indications of security problems, such as repeated unsuccessful attempts to log-on the computer system or to access protected files.

Log records can be used to help detect, for example, automatic access attempts using systematic password variations. Log records also indicate computer-security program quality. For example, passwords that are changed too frequently may confuse users about which password is currently effective. It is also important to tell users—either formally or informally—when the password change will take effect. A successful notification process will result in fewer incorrect access attempts.

Password Pickup

Passwords are intended to be private. They should not be divulged to anyone. However, some users are careless; they write passwords on blackboards or desk pads or leave password issue cards exposed on desks or other readily accessible places.

An extremely useful technique for companies with security guard forces is to request that guards turn over exposed passwords found during routine patrol to the computer-security or password-control organization on the grounds that if they were available to the guard they could have been exposed to others. Such compromised passwords should be disabled and their users required to apply for a new password.

This procedure has two benefits. Users quickly become aware of their responsibility to protect passwords and the computer-security organization can collect data on users' awareness of their responsibilities.

Incident Reporting

One of the best indicators (although certainly not foolproof) of a computer-security program's success is the history of the violations discovered. A case history of incidents frequently includes problems uncovered by accident rather than by design. Although a vigilant computer-security program will include monitoring designed to detect problems and incidents, such data would mostly reflect only incidents that were anticipated. Accidental discoveries are also clearly important. Data should be compiled only for specific programs for two reasons. First, the data reflect more accurately an assessment of the particular program of interest. Second, many incidents are discussed within a company and not outside. That is, companies sometimes do not wish to publicize an incident out of embarrassment or because knowledge of the incident might reflect a poor image of effective management. Such companies sometimes fear that publicity could result in a libel suit by the accused person. Even when a company does not attempt to suppress knowledge of a security violation, it frequently has no prescribed mechanism for reporting or recording such incidents.

Security Tests

Security tests (discussed in an earlier chapter as an aid in establishing procedural controls) are also useful in evaluating security. Security tests will sometimes reveal uncorrected vulnerabilities. These weaknesses have been justified for a number of reasons, ranging from financial and user efficiency to the refusal to believe that they are noteworthy.

The vulnerabilities found in a security-test program can be evaluated in two ways. First, a large number of vulnerabilities requiring corrective action may indicate weaknesses in the original security plans, as well as the probability of remaining unidentified vulnerabilities. Second, a large number of uncorrected vulnerabilities may reflect overall security weakness that might well be exploited.

Data Analysis

Risk analysis was discussed in chapter 6 as a method of determining cost-effective computer-security safeguards. The main value of risk analysis is usually considered to be this "before-the-fact" selection. Risk analysis can also be a powerful after-the-fact assessment tool applied to various computer-security measures. In fact, it can even be applied to the risk-analysis program to measure its effectiveness.

One of the best ways to apply this type of analysis is the consistent gathering of data that can be converted to assessment measures. When audits are made, compilations of citations can be accumulated. When files are monitored and logs are examined, statistics on the results are valuable. When security guards pick up passwords, quantities and locations can be indicators. Breaches of security provide additional statistics for risk analysis. Risk analysis indicates the necessary security changes in each of these situations. The time required to establish and implement the features of the security program should be budgeted in each type of risk analysis.

The analyses discussed in this chapter should, if properly done, provide a useful evaluation of computer security, including indicators of the major weaknesses and successes. They can also indicate the balance point between protection and operational efficiency, which should never swing strongly to one side or the other in a carefully planned computer-security program.

Selecting Appropriate Techniques

The final important question is how to select the techniques described in this book to formulate a computer-security program. Unfortunately, neither this book nor any other source can provide complete information because computer security must be highly individualized for each program and for each installation. In addition, prescribed steps generally provide more protection against accidents and casual mischief than against an intent criminal.

This book does provide some guidance in selecting a direction to pursue, however. First, every known technique should be given at least cursory consideration. Too hasty dismissal can mean missing important opportunities for effective safeguards. Second, at least some form of risk analysis is helpful in making these decisions. The importance of using cost-effective safeguards cannot be overemphasized. Consultants—either peers or contractors—provide the combined advantages of special expertise and a different or fresh viewpoint of the situation. Finally, a comprehensive literature reference collection (books, periodicals, reports) stimulates new ideas and balanced evaluations effectively.

Appendix A
Technology Suppliers

Appendix A is an alphabetical listing of some of the vendors that have relevant computer-security technology. Appendix B lists vendors organized by several types of technology.

Information in the lists of technology suppliers was obtained from vendor brochures, books, and various buyers' guides, including the *1980 Computer Security Buyers' Guide* (published by the Computer Security Institute Press, Hudson, MA and *Who, What, and Where in Communications Security* published by Marketing Consultants International Inc., Hagerstown, MD). Although the information in this appendix is intended to be up to date, accurate, and comprehensive as of the publication date, it carries no warranties. It is intended only as a guide for initiating contacts. No slight of any vendor was intended.

Access Control Systems
2105 S. Hardy Dr.
Tempe, AZ 85282
(602) 966-3086

AC Manufacturing Co.
Old Cuthbert and Deer Roads
Cherry Hill, NJ 08034
(609) 428-9800

ADC
1160 Chestnut St.
Menlo Park, CA 94025
(415) 323-1386

ADR/Datacom
3703 Rawlins St.
Dallas TX 75219
(214) 526-4280

Advance Conversion Devices
109 8th St.
Passaic, NJ 07055
(207) 778-0707

Advanced Information
Management Inc.
1988 Opitz Blvd.
Woodbridge, VA 22191
(800) 368-3144

Allegheny Business Systems Inc.
P.O. Drawer E
Delmont, PA 15626
(800) 245-2497

Allen Services Corp.
4175 Mercantile Ave.
Naples, FL 33942
(813) 774-3077

American Satellite Corp.
20301 Century Blvd.
Germantown, MD 20767
(301) 428-6040

Ampex
401G Broadway
Redwood City, CA 94404
(415) 367-2011

The Ansul Company
1 Stanton St.
Marinette, WI 54143
(715) 735-7411

Applied Digital Data Systems Inc.
100G Marcus Blvd.
Hauppauge, NY 11788
(516) 231-5400

Applied Software, Inc.
4440 P.G.A. Boulevard, Suite 204
Palm Beach Gardens, FL 33410
(305) 626-4818

Arbat Systems Limited
Arbat Plaza
Hoboken, NJ 07030
(201) 963-4440

Atlas Energy Systems
9457 Rush St.
S. El Monte, CA 91733
(213) 575-0755

Avanti Communications Corp.
Dept. G, Aquidneck Industrial Park
Newport, RI 02840
(401) 849-4660

Baird Info-Systems Safeguards Inc.
98 Crestview Rd.
Mountain Lakes, NJ 07046
(201) 334-5626

Bekaert Steel Wire Corp.
800 Third Ave.
New York, NY 10022
(212) 371-4240

Belden Corp.
2000 S. Batavia Ave.
Geneva, IL 60134
(312) 232-8900

Bell and Howell
360G Sierra Madre Villa
Pasadena, CA 91109
(213) 796-9381

Bi-Hex Co.
P.O. Box 312
Bedford Village, NY 10506
(914) 764-4021

Black Box Catalog
P.O. Box 12800
Pittsburg, PA 15241
(412) 746-2910

Blazer Industries
700 21st Ave.
Patterson, NJ 07513
(201) 881-9110

Boole & Babbage Inc.
510 Oakmead Parkway
Sunnyvale, CA 94086
(408) 735-9550

Booz-Allen
4330 East West Highway
Bethesda, MD 20014
(301) 951-2200

Brandt Allen
P.O. Box 6550
Charlottesville, VA 22906
(804) 924-7486

Burns International Security
Services Inc.
320 Buffalo Rd.
Briarcliff Manor, NY 10510
(914) 762-1000

Cambridge Systems Group
24275 Elise
Los Altos Hills, CA 94022
(415) 941-4558

Canoga Data Systems
21218 Vanowen St.
Canoga Park, CA 91303
(213) 888-2003

Cardkey Systems
20660 Bahama St.
Chatsworth, CA 91311
(213) 882-8111

CGA Software Products Group, Inc.
212 West National Rd.
Vandalia, OH 45377
(513) 890-1200

Chemetron
Governor's Highway & Route 50
Monee, IL 60449
(312) 534-1000

Chicago Data Systems Inc.
2805 Butterfield Rd.
Oak Brook, IL 60521
(312) 325-2960

Chubb Industries Inc.
411 Feheley Dr.
King of Prussia, PA 19406
(215) 277-3010

Citibank, N.A.
P.O. Box 1127
153 East 53rd St.
New York, NY 10043
(212) 559-4421

Clary Corp.
320 W. Clary Ave.
San Gabriel, CA 91776
(213) 287-6111

Codex
20G Cabot Blvd.
Mansfield, MA 02048
(617) 367-2000

Collins Telecommunications Products
Electronic Systems Group
P.O. Box 728
Cedar Rapids, IA 52406
(319) 395-1000

Columbia National
General Agency
88 East Broad St.
Columbus, OH 43215
(800) 848-0598

Comdata
7900 N. Nagle Ave.
Morton Grove, IL 60053
(312) 470-9600

ComDesign
751 S. Kellogg Ave.
Goleta, CA 93117
(805) 964-9852

Comdisco Disaster Recovery
Services, Inc.
6400 Shafer Court
Rosemont, IL 60018
(312) 698-3000

Communication Control Systems Ltd.
605 Third Ave.
New York, NY 10016
(212) 683-4637

Comparator Systems Corporation
1900 E. Ocean Blvd., Suite 1803
Long Beach, CA 90802
(213) 437-4040

Computer Consulting by Konigsford
99 Montell
Piedmont, CA 94611
(415) 549-2152

Computer Infomatrix Inc.
10850 Wilshire
Los Angeles, CA 90024
(213) 475-9876

Computer Link Corp.
40G Ray Ave.
Burlington, MA 01803
(617) 272-7400

Computer Power Inc.
124 W. Main St.
High Bridge, NJ 08829
(201) 735-8000

Computer Research Co.
200 N. Michigan Ave.
Chicago, IL 60601
(312) 977-7500

Computer Resource Controls Inc.
17 West Jefferson St.
Rockville, MD 20850
(301) 340-9818

Continental Instruments Corp.
70G Hopper St.
Westbury, NY 11590
(516) 938-0800

Contingency Group Inc.
P.O. Box 257
Bensenville, IL 60106
(312) 860-1650

Corporate Contingency Services
P.O. Box 805
New Hudson, MI 48165
(313) 486-2110

CPT Corporation
8100 Mitchell Road
Minneapolis, MN 55440
(612) 937-8000

Crown Industries
2100 Commerce Dr.
Fremont, OH 43420
(419) 332-5531

Cullinet Software
400 Blue Hill Dr.
Westwood, MA 02090
(617) 329-7700

Cummins-Allison Corp.
4740 North Ravenswood
Chicago, IL 60640
(312) 989-3700

Cyberex Inc.
7171 Industrial Park Blvd.
Mentor, OH 44060
(216) 946-1783

Data Plus Inc.
1218 Massachusetts Ave.
Cambridge, MA 02138
(617) 547-4875

Data Processing Security Inc.
200 E. Loop 820
Ft. Worth, TX 76112
(817) 457-9400

Data Products Corp.
Barnes Park North
Wallingford, CT 06492
(203) 265-7151

DataCode
5122 St. Clair Ave.
Cleveland, OH 44193
(216) 881-2100

Dataguard Corporate Office
2050 Center Avenue
Fort Lee, NJ 07024
(201) 592-7868

Datashield Inc.
P.O. Box 242
Greendale, WI 53129
(414) 421-7710

Datatech Business Machines
8370 Mountain Sights Ave.
Montreal, Quebec
Canada 2B3
(514) 735-5356

Dektor Counterintelligence and
Security Inc.
5508 Port Royal Rd.
Springfield, VA 22151
(703) 321-9333

Denco Corp.
P.O. Box 1442
Rockville, MD 20850
(301) 948-2090

Devlin Associates
1150 First Ave., Suite 795
King of Prussia, PA 19406
(215) 337-1667

Devoke Co.
3780 Fabian Way
Palo Alto, CA 94303
(415) 494-8844

Digilog Inc.
1370 Welsh Road
Montgomeryville, PA 18936
(215) 628-4530

Document Disintegration Systems
2075 Belgrave Ave.
Hungtington Park, CA 90255
(213) 588-2231

Don White Consultants Inc.
P.O. Box D
Gainsville, VA 22065
(703) 347-0030

Dorlen Products
7424 W. Layton Ave.
Greenfield, WI 53220
(414) 282-4840

Dylakor
17418 Chatsworth St.
Granada Hills, CA 91344
(213) 366-1781

EDP Audit Controls, Inc.
7700 Edgewater Dr.
Oakland, CA 94621
(415) 638-4075

EDS Software Products
7171 Forest Lane
Dallas, TX 75230
(800) 527-0128

E.I. du Pont de Nemours & Co. Inc.
Freon Products Laboratory
Chestnut Run
Wilmington, DE 19898
(302) 774-2566

Electric Wastebasket Corp.
145 W. 45th St.
New York, NY 10036
(212) 997-1700

Emerson Electric
3300 S. Standard St.
Santa Ana, CA 92702
(714) 545-5581

Emidata Systems
9800 Reistertown Rd.
Garrison, MD 21055
(301) 363-1600

EMP Corporation
9616 Owensmouth Avenue
Chatsworth, CA 91311
(213) 882-6333

Exide Electronics
2 Penn Center Plaza
Philadelphia, PA 19102
(215) 422-4000

Exide Power Conversion
3301 Spring Forest Rd.
Raleigh, NC 27604
(919) 872-3020

Eyedentify, Inc.
1225 N.W. Murray Road
Portland, OR 97229
(503) 644-9838

Fact Finders Inc.
458 Springfield Ave.
Summit, NJ 07901
(201) 522-0220

Fenwal Inc.
400 Main Street
Ashland, MA 01721
(617) 881-2000

Filegard Systems
4440 PGA Blvd., Suite 204
Palm Beach Gardens, FL 33410
(305) 626-4818

Fingermatrix, Inc.
30 Virginia Road
No. White Plains, NY 10603
(914) 428-5441

Fiquench
Fire Suppression Systems
P.O. Box 610
Blue Springs, MO 64015
(816) 229-3405

Fireman's Fund Insurance Companies
3333 California St.
San Francisco, CA 94119
(415) 929-2000

Firetek Corp.
53 Thomas Rd.
Hawthorne, NJ 07506
(201) 427-9804

Franklin Electric
995 Benicia Ave.
Sunnyvale, CA 94086
(800) 538-1770

Gandalf Data
1019 South Noel St.
Wheeling, IL 60090
(312) 541-6060

General Electric Company
Communications Equipment Services
Building 4, Room 210
1 River Road
Schenectady, NY 12345
(518) 385-0551

General Kinetics, Inc.
12300 Parklawn Dr.
Rockville, MD 20852
(301) 881-2044

Graviner Inc.
1121 Bristol Rd.
Mountainside, NJ 07092
(201) 654-6800

Hansco Data Processing Inc.
P.O. Box 236
Wilbraham, MA 01095
(413) 732-9613

Hewlett Packard
3000 Hanover St.
Palo Alto, CA 94304
(415) 857-1501

Hiross Incorporated
P.O. Box 290 LPO
2107 Libert Drive
Niagara Falls, NY 14304
(716) 283-6464

Holmes Protection Inc.
370 Seventh Ave.
New York, NY 10001
(212) 868-5676

Honeywell Commercial Branch
10800 Lyndale Ave. South
Bloomington, MN 55420
(612) 887-4049

Hosman Associates Inc.
10602 Lakespring Way
Cockeysville, MD 21030
(301) 667-0453

IBM Corporation
P.O. Box 218
Yorktown Heights, NY 10598
(914) 945-1462

ICI Americas Inc.
Wilmington, DE 19897
(302) 575-3538

ICS Inc.
520 Interstate Rd.
Addison, IL 60101
(312) 543-6200

Identimat Corp.
135 West 50th Street
New York, NY 10020
(212) 371-3300

Ikegami Electronics (USA) Inc.
29-19 39th Avenue
Long Island City, NY 11101
(212) 932-2577

Industrial Shredder & Cutter Co.
707 S. Ellsworth Ave.
Salem, OHS 44460
(216) 332-0024

Informatics Inc.
21050 Vanowen St.
Canoga Park, CA 91304
(213) 887-9121

Interstate Electronics, Inc.
101 East Ball Road
Anaheim, CA 92803
(714) 635-7210

International Mobile Machines
Corporation
100 N. 20th St.
Philadelphia, PA 19103
(215) 569-1300

International Power Machines Corp.
P.O. Box 724
3328 Executive Blvd.
Mesquite, TX 75149
(214) 288-7501

Jerry Fitzgerald & Associates
506 Barkentine Lane
Redwood City, CA 94065
(415) 591-5676

Jobmaster Corp.
9010 Liberty Rd.
Randallstown, MD 21133
(301) 655-1400

Jones Futurex Inc.
9700 Fair Oaks Blvd., Suite G
Fair Oaks, CA 95628
(916) 966-6836

K-F Industries Inc.
230 West Dauphin St.
Philadelphia, PA 19133
(215) 425-7710

Laminex Inc.
600 Matthews-Mint Hill Rd.
P.O. Box 577
Matthews, NC 28105
(704) 847-9143

Lance J. Hoffman
2746 Woodley Pl. NW
Washington, DC 20008
(202) 332-9363

Lanier Business Products
1700 Chantilly Drive NE
Atlanta, GA 30324
(404) 329-8000

Lexitron Corporation
(see Raytheon Data Systems)

Liebert Corp.
1050 Dearborn Dr.
Columbus, OH 43229
(614) 888-0246

Lightning Elimination Associates
12516 Lakeland Rd.
Santa Fe Springs, CA 90670
(213) 944-0916

Management & Computer Services Inc.
790 Valley Forge
P.O. Box 826
Valley Forge, PA 19482
(215) 648-0730

Mastiff Systems, U.S., Inc.
Pleasantdale Business Center
4029 Pleasantdale Rd., Suite 545
Atlanta, GA 30340
(404) 448-4100

Marsh & McLennan
1221 Avenue of the Americas
New York, NY 10020
(212) 997-7000

Medeco
P.O. Box 1075
Salem, VA 24153
(703) 387-0481

Mellonics Information Center
6701 Variel Ave.
Canoga Park, CA 91303
(213) 716-2240

Micropad, Inc.
5650 S. Brainard Avenue
La Grange, IL 60525
(312) 579-3200

MIS Associates
12 Jupiter Lane
Framingham, MA 01701
(617) 879-7999

Mosler Airmatic & Electronic
Systems Division
415 Hamburg Turnpike
Wayne, NJ 07470
(201) 595-4000

Motorola Communications and
Electronics
1301 E. Algonquin Rd.
Schaumberg, IL 60196
(312) 397-1000

NCI Inc.
3720 Longview Dr.
Atlanta, GA 30341
(404) 451-7455

North American Video
5 Granite Road
Acton, MA 01720
(617) 263-6700

Nova Electric Manufacturing Co.
263 Hillside Ave.
Nutley, NJ 07110
(201) 661-3434

Novatec Corporation
P.O. Box 1508, Dept. G
Sanford, NC 27330
(919) 775-7318

NUSAC Inc.
7926 Jones Branch Dr.
McLean, VA 22102
(703) 893-6004

On-Line Software International
65 Route 4 East
River Edge, NJ 07661
(201) 488-7770

Opticode Inc.
2745 Lafitte Street
New Orleans, LA 70119
(504) 486-6222

Palmguard
12810 SW Canyon Rd.
Beaverton, OR 97005
(503) 644-3235

Panasonic Company
One Panasonic Way
Secaucus, NJ 07094
(201) 348-52259

Pansophic Systems Inc.
709 Enterprise Dr.
Oak Brook, IL 60521
(312) 986-6055

Perey Turnstiles
101 Park Ave.
New York, NY 10017
(212) 679-6080

William E. Perry & Associates
5 Sleepy Hollow Cove
Longwood, FL 32750
(305) 830-1594

Power Dynamics Corp.
177 Valley
S. Orange, NJ 07079
(201) 762-6886

Precision Methods Inc.
3510 S. Congress Ave., Suite 4
Austin, TX 78704
(512) 443-9575

Preso-Matic Lock Company Inc.
3048 Industrial 33rd St.
Fort Pierce, FL 33450
(305) 465-7400

Printrak, Inc.
2121 S. Manchester Avenue
Anaheim, CA 92801
(714) 634-1872

Pro-Net Inc.
14940B 28th Ave. North
Plymouth, MN 55441
(612) 559-7284

Program Products Inc.
95 Chestnut Ridge Rd.
Montvale, NJ 07645
(201) 391-9800

Protective Services
P.O. Box 3392
Modesto, CA 95353
(209) 577-5929

Pyrotronics
8 Ridgedale Ave.
Cedar Knolls, NJ 07927
(201) 267-1300

Quality Systems Development Corp.
645 N. Michigan Ave. Suite 638
Chicago, IL 60611
(312) 266-6060

Racal-Vadic
222 Caspian Dr.
Sunnyvale, CA 94086
(408) 744-0810

RAH Associates
P.O. Box 71
Maplewood, NJ 07040
(201) 761-7555

Randolph Engineering
P.O. Box 3272
3810 Manchaw Rd.
Austin, TX 78764
(512) 442-3584

Raytheon Data Systems
1415 Boston-Providence Turnpike
Norwood, MA 02062
(617) 762-6700

RCA
Closed Circuit Video Equipment
New Holland Ave.
Lancaster, PA 17604
(717) 397-7661

Receptors Inc.
4203 Spencer St.
Torrance, CA 90503
(213) 542-0501

Resdel Engineering Corp.
300 E. Live Oak Ave.
Arcadia, CA 91006
(213) 445-5955

Retawmatic Corp.
505 5th Ave.
Box 460 Grand Central Station
New York, NY 10017
(212) 687-0890

RKS Industries Inc.
4865 Scotts Valley Drive
Scotts Valley, CA 95066
(408) 438-5760

Robert Courtney Inc.
Box 836
Port Ewen, NY 12466
(914) 338-2525

Robertshaw Controls Co.
333 N. Euclid Way
Anaheim, CA 92803
(714) 535-8151

Robot Industries Inc.
7041 Orchard St.
Dearborn, MI 48126
(313) 846-2623

Rusco Electronic Systems
1840 Victory Blvd.
Glendale, CA 91201
(213) 240-2540

Russelectric, Inc.
South Shore Industrial Park
Hingham, MA 02043
(617) 749-6000

Saber Laboratories Inc.
577 Tenth St.
San Francisco, CA 94103
(415) 431-4707

St. Paul Fire and Marine
Insurance Co.
385 Washington St.
St. Paul, MN 55102
(612) 221-7911

Sargent & Greenleaf
1 Security Drive
Nicholasville, KY 40356
(606) 885-9411

Schlage Electronics
3260 Scott Blvd.
Santa Clara CA 95051
(408) 727-5170

SDI
P.O. Box 5801
San Mateo, CA 94403
(415) 572-1200

Secom
8703 La Tijera Blvd.
Los Angeles, CA 90045
(213) 641-1290

Security Consultants International
400 Durham Dr.
Houston, TX 77007
(713) 868-1511

Security Engineered Machinery
5 Walkup Dr.
Westboro, MA 01581
(800) 225-9293

SG2
8350 N. Central Expressway #1178
Dallas, TX 75206
(214) 368-2902

Shredmaster Corp.
22030 W. McNab Rd.
Ft. Lauderdale, FL 33309
(305) 974-6500

Siecor Corporation
489 Siecor Park
Hickory, NC 28601
(704) 328-2171

Simplex Security Systems, Inc.
Front & Main Streets
Collinsville, CT 06022
(203) 693-8391

Skandia Insurance Co. Ltd.
S-103 50
Stockholm Sweden

Software Solutions Inc.
26 Computer Dr. East
Albany, NY 12205
(518) 458-1860

Sorenson Company
676 Island Pond Rd.
Manchester, NH 03103
(603) 668-4500

SRI International
333 Ravenswood Ave.
Menlo Park, CA 94025
(415) 326-6400

Stasis
4 Vanderbilt
South Irvine, CA 92714
(714) 770-5397

Stellar Systems
231 Charcot Ave.
San Jose, CA 95131
(408) 946-6460

Stelma Telecommunications
17 Amelia Place
Stamford, CT 06902
(203) 265-7151

Sun Information Services Co.
10 Penn Center, 8th Floor
1801 Market St.
Philadelphia, PA 19103
(215) 972-4219

Superior Electric Co.
383 Middle St.
Bristol, CT 06010
(203) 582-9461

Synergistics, Inc.
10 Huron Dr.
Natick, MA 01760
(617) 655-1340

Systematics General Corp.
National Scientific Labs Div.
2922 Telestar Court
Falls Church, VA 22042
(703) 698-8500

Systematics Incorporated
41 Colonial Drive
Piscataway, NJ 08845
(201) 981-1300

Technical Analysis Corp.
120 W. Wieuca Road NE
Atlanta, GA 30042
(404) 252-1045

Texas Instruments
13510 N. Central Expressway
P.O. Box 225214, Mail Station 394
Dallas, TX 75265
(214) 995-3977

Theodore M. Schwartz and
Associates, Inc.
15 Stewart Place
White Plains, NY 10601
(914) 681-0177

The 3M Company
Static Control Systems
3M Center, Bldg. 223-2s
St. Paul, MN 55101
(612) 733-3285

Threshold Technology, Inc.
1829 Underwood Boulevard
Delran, NJ 08075
(609) 461-9200

Time-Lock-Inc.
87 Water Mill Lane
Great Neck, NY 11021
(516) 487-0690

Tower Systems, Inc.
19782 MacArthur Blvd., Suite 365
Irvine, CA 92715
(800) 854-7551

Toye Corporation
P.O. Box 729
Chatsworth, CA 91311
(213) 882-4000

The Trane Company
3600 Pammel Creek Rd.
La Crosse, WI 54601
(608) 787-3111

Transaction Security Ltd.
P.O. Box 72, Barratt House
Chestnut Avenue
Guildford, Surrey
GU2 5HJ England
(0483) 503363

United Technical Products Inc.
23 Southwest Industrial Park
Westwood, MA 02090
(617) 326-7611

Versitron, Inc.
6310 Chillum Pl. NW
Washington, DC 20011
(202) 882-8464

Vikonics Inc.
23-25 East 26th St.
New York, NY 10010
(212) 686-4152

Visual Methods Inc.
35 Charles St.
Westwood, NJ 07675
(201) 666-3950

VM Software Inc.
P.O. Box 985
Vienna, VA 22180
(703) 821-6886

Votan
4487 Technology Drive
Fremont, CA 94538
(415) 490-7600

Wackenhut Electronic Systems Corp.
1742 NW 69th Avenue
Miami, FL 33126
(305) 592-3278

Walter Kidde & Co.
675 Main St.
Belleville, NJ 07109
(201) 759-5000

Wang Laboratories
1 Industrial Ave.
Lowell, MA 01851
(617) 459-5000

Welco Industries Inc.
9027 Shell Rd.
Cincinnati, OH 45236
(513) 891-6600

Westinghouse Electric
P.O. Box 225
Buffalo, NY 14240
(716) 631-2413

Wilson Jones Co.
6150 Touhy Ave.
Chicago, IL 60648
(312) 774-7700

Worlen Products
7424 W. Layton Ave.
Greenfield WI 53220
(414) 282-4840

Xerox Corporation
Office Systems Division
1341 West Mockingbird Lane
Dallas, TX 75247
(214) 689-6000

Appendix B
Vendor Categories

Contents

Tempest Protection

Uninterruptible Power Systems

Water Detection

Access Control Hardware

Cardkey Systems
Comparator Systems Corporation
Devoke Co.
Continental Instruments Corp.
DataCode
Datakey
Emidata/Malco
EMP Corporation
Eyedentify, Inc.
Filegard Systems
Fingermatrix Inc.
IBM Corporation
Identimat
International Mobile Machines Corp.
Laminex
Mastiff Systems, U.S., Inc.
Medeco
Micropad, Inc.
Mosler Airmatic &
Electronic Systems Division
Opticode Inc.
Palmguard, Inc.
Perey Turnstiles
Preso-Matic Lock Company Inc.
Printrak, Inc.
Pro-Net Inc.
Robot Industries Inc.
Rusco Electronic Systems
Sarget & Greenleaf
Schlage Electronics
Stasis
Secom
Simplex Security Systems Inc.
Stellar Systems
Synergistics Inc.
Systematics Incorporated
Texas Instruments
Threshold Technology, Inc.
Time-Lock Inc.
Transaction Security, Ltd.
Toye Corporation
Vikonics Inc.
Visual Methods Inc.
Votan
Wackenhut Electronic Systems Corp.

Air Conditioning

AC Manufacturing Co.
Blazer Industries

Hiross Incorporated
Liebert Corp.
The Trane Company

Audit Software

Citibank, N.A.
Computer Informatrix Inc.
Cullinet Software
Dylakor
EDP Audit Controls Inc.
Informatics Inc.
Management & Computer Services Inc.
NCI Inc.
Pansophic Systems Inc.
Program Products Inc.

Closed-Circuit TV

Ikegam Electronics (USA) Inc.
North American Video
Panasonic Company
RCA

Consultants

Access Control Systems
Advanced Information
Management Inc.
Baird Info-Systems Safeguards Inc.
Bi-Hex Co.
Booz-Allen
Brandt Allen
Burns International Security
Services Inc.
Computer Consulting by Konigsford
Computer Resource Controls Inc.
Corporate Contingency Services
Data Plus Inc.
Devlin Associates
EDP Audit Controls Inc.
Fact Finders Inc.
Jerry Fitzgerald & Associates
Lance J. Hoffman
Hosman Associates Inc.
Marsh & McLennan
MIS Associates
Nusac Inc.
On-Line Software International
Protective Services
RAH Associates
Randolph Engineering

Robert Courtney Inc.
Security Consultants International
SG2
SRI International
Theodore M. Schwartz and
Associates, Inc.
William E. Perry & Associates

Data Communications

ADC
Avanti Communications Corp.
Black Box Catalog
Bo-Sherrel Co.
Codex
Com Data
ComDesign
Dataproducts
Digilog Inc.
Gandalf Data Inc.
General Electric Company
Racal-Vadic
Stelma Communications
Technical Analysis Corp.

Degaussers

Ampex
Bell and Howell
Computer Link Corp.
General Kinetics Inc.
Hewlett Packard
Jobmaster Corp.
Precision Methods Inc.

ECM/EMI

Communication Control Systems Ltd.
Dektor Counterintelligence and
Security Inc.
Don White Consultants Inc.

Encryption Hardware

American Satellite Corp.
Codex
Collins Telecommunications Products
Jones Futurex Inc.
Resdel Engineering Corp.
Saber Laboratories Inc.

Encryption Software

ADR Datacom
Applied Software, Inc.
Bi-Hex Co.
Hansco Data Processing Inc.
Informatics Inc.
Software Solutions Inc.

Fiber Optics Peripherals

Belden Corp.
Canoga Data Systems
Siecor Corporation
Versitron, Inc.

Fire Detection/Suppression Systems

The Ansul Co.
Chemetron Corp.
E.I. du Pont de Nemours & Co. Inc.
Fenwall Inc.
Fiquench
Firetek Corp.
Graviner Inc.
ICI Americas Inc.
Pyrotronics
Walter Kidde & Co.

General Security

Burns International Security
Services Inc.
Chubb Industries Inc.
Motorola Communications &
Electronics
Receptors Inc.
Robertshaw Controls Inc.

Insurance

Columbia National
Fireman's Fund Insurance Companies
St. Paul Fire and Marine
Insurance Co.
Skandia Insurance Co. Ltd.

Lightning/Electrical Protection

Lightning Elimination Associates Inc.
Superior Electric

Recovery/Backup Facilities

Arbat Systems Limited
Comdisco Disaster Recovery
Services, Inc.
Computer Research Co.
Contingency Group Inc.
Corporate Contingency Services
Data Processing Security Inc.
Dataguard Corporate Office
Datashield Inc.
Devlin Associates, Inc.
Mellonics Information Center
Sun Information Services Co.
VM Software Inc.

Security Software

Allen Services Corp.
Applied Software, Inc.
Boole and Babbage Inc.
Cambridge Systems Group
CGA Software Products Group Inc.
Chicago Data Systems Inc.
EDS Software Products
Electronic Data Systems Corp.
Informatics Inc.
On-Line Software International
Pansophic Systems Inc.
Quality Systems Development Corp.
SDI
Tower Systems, Inc.

Shredders

Allegheny Business Systems Inc.
Cummins-Allison Corp.
Datatech Business Machines
Devoke Data Products
Document Disintegration Systems
Electric Wastebasket Corp.
Industrial Shredder and Cutter Co.
Novatec Corporation
Security Engineered Machinery
Shredmaster Corp.
Wilson Jones Co.

Static Electricity Suppression

Bekaert Steel Wire Corp.

Crown Industries
The 3M Company Static Control
Systems
United Technical Products Inc.

Tempest Protection

CPT Corp.
Dataproducts Corp.
IBM
Lanier Business Products
Raytheon Data Systems
Systematics General Corp.
Teletype Corp.
Wang Laboratories
Xerox Corp.

Uninterruptible Power Systems

Advance Conversion Devices
Atlas Energy Systems
Clary Corp.
Computer Power Inc.
Cyberex Inc.
Emerson Electric Co.
Exide Electronics
Exide Power Conversion
Franklin Electric
ICS Inc.
International Power Machines Corp.
Nova Electric Manufacturing Co.
Power Dynamics Corp.
RKS Industries, Inc.
Russelectric, Inc.
Sorenson Company
The Superior Electric Co.
Welco Industries Inc.
Westinghouse Electric

Water Detection

Denco Corp.
Dorlen Products
K-F Industries Inc.
Retawmatic Corp.

Glossary

Access controls Techniques restricting access to a physical area or to a computer so that only authorized users are allowed.

Access matrix A systematic set of rules showing the rights (such as read, write) a specific user has for a particular object (such as files).

ACK Acknowledge.

Acoustic coupler Device for coupling electrical data lines to acoustic telephones for transmission through telephone system.

ACU Automatic calling units.

ADCCP Advanced data-communications control procedure.

ADP Administrative data processing, or automatic data processing.

AFC Automatic frequency control for locking onto FM signals.

AGC Automatic gain control for stabilizing amplitude variations in a received signal.

Algorithm Specified series of steps for accomplishing a prescribed function.

ALOHA A network broadcast system, in which every station has the capability to broadcast and receive from every other station, with the broadcast simultaneous to as many stations as desired.

AM Amplitude modulation—that is, variations in amplitude of a "carrier" frequency to convey the information; adaptive multiplexer.

Analog loopback Diagnostic check by connecting analog transmitter output to receiver input.

Ancestor A node in a tree structure with one or more descendants.

APC Adaptive predictive coding.

APD (avalanche photodiode) A receiving device in fiber-optics systems.

Application programmer Responsible for design, development, testing, documentation and maintenance of programs for user applications.

Applications software Programs designed by users to accomplish specific tasks for the users.

Architecture Basic system implementation or connection of standard modules.

ARPANET Department of Defense packet-switching computer network.

ARQ Automatic retransmission request.

Arrester A nonlinear device for suppressing voltage transients that result from lightning, power surges, or other power problems.

ASCII code An 8-bit code for alphanumeric characters commonly used by terminals and similar instruments.

Assembly language   Representation of machine language that gives the programmer easier use by mnemonic represention of instruction bit patterns and memory locations.

Asymmetric cryptosystem   Separate keys for encryption and decryption.

Asynchronous   Data or signals that occur in response to an initiating source without any waiting for a clock time.

ATM (automatic teller machine)   A station where bank transactions can be made by terminal entries following validation of the user's code entered on the keyboard.

Audit   Independent review and examination of records.

Audit trail   Chronological record allowing reconstruction of events.

Authentication   Verifying that a message came from the expected source.

Autodialer   An automatic phone-signaling device that can be used to simulate number dialing.

Autokey cipher   Key derived from the message it enciphers.

Automatic calling unit (autodialer)   Device or capability for generating dial or touch-tone signals under programmed control for establishing telephone connection.

Automatic disconnects   A switching system than can be applied to telephone circuits so that the circuit is disconnected some distance from the telephone (the circuit between the telephone and the disconnect is completely inactive). This prevents unintended energy from equipment near the telephone from being coupled onto telephone circuits. Picking up the receiver enables the circuit.

Autotransformer   A variable transformer providing no isolation because the primary and secondary share common windings.

Asynchronous   Each character has a start symbol and a stop symbol.

Backup   Method of ensuring maintenance of essential capabilities in the event that crucial facilities or data are lost.

Baseband   A local area network communication technique where the data are entered directly onto the transmission medium with no frequency conversion.

Batch   Large volume data transmission or noninteractive sequences of program execution.

Baud   Symbols-per-second communication rate.

Baudot code   A 5-bit code for alphanumeric data often used in digital-communication devices.

Baud rate   Signaling intelligence per unit time. Bits of information conveyed may be at a higher rate than the baud rate.

BCF (bromochlorodifluoromethane)   ($CBrClF_2$). Also known as Halon 1211, BCF is a gas used for fire suppression.

BEC   Burst error codes.

Bell modems   The standard modems introduced by the phone company.
BER   Bit error rate.
Bit   Binary digit (zero or one).
Blackout   Complete loss of power.
Block chaining   Insertion of bits from previous ciphertext before enciphering current block of information.
Block cipher   Blocks of data, each encrypted in the same key.
Blocking   Communication prevented because the interconnection is busy or one of the parties is already communicating elsewhere.
Boolean operations   Logical operations such as AND, OR, NOT, exclusive-OR.
Boot   To insert the software into a computer system that will control its operation.
Bootstrap loader   Loader that loads itself into memory after a key instruction or instructions (called a "bootstrap") has been inserted (or read out of ROM).
bps   bits per second.
Broadband   Local network technique for translating data to relatively high modulated frequency so that the link can be shared by multiple communications possibly taking place at multiple frequencies.
Brownout   Power reduction due to excessive load.
BSC   Bisync, half duplex.
Bubble memory   Memory using microscopic magnetic domains in an aluminum-garnet substrate.
Buffer   Temporary storage for data that allows insertion and removal under separate synchronization control.
Buffered   Read into buffer by a source clock and out of buffer by a sink clock.
Bus   A connection medium to which multiple nodes may be connected. The nodes are essentially independent from other node connections, but can communicate with the other nodes.
Bus network   A network interconnection topology that provides node connection to a communication medium (bus) independent of any other connections to the bus, so that any node can communicate with any other node.
Bypass   Allowing plaintext information to pass around an encryption device without any coding.
Byte   Group (usually 8) of binary digits (bits).

Cable   Stranded assembly of electrical conductors twisted around a central core—usually heavily insulated by outside wrappings.
Cache   High-speed memory used as a buffer between main memory and the CPU.

Carrier   An AC signal that can be modulated in various ways to carry information.

Cassette   Small cartridge, usually containing 1/4-in magnetic tape, used for microcomputer mass storage.

CBC   Cipher block chaining.

CCTV (closed-circuit television)   Remote observation device of areas requiring protection.

CCITT (Consultative Committee of International Telephone and Telegraph)   The body responsible for the widely used packet transmission protocol X.25.

CD (conditioned diphase)   A diphase signal with data and clock contained in same signal.

Cellular radio   Programmable, scanning, frequency-synthesized units that transmit and receive data and FM signals.

Central computer facility   A centralized powerful computing capability that multiple users can share.

Central processing unit (CPU)   Sequential logic circuitry containing arithmetic logic units, instruction decoding circuitry, timing and control circuits, temporary storage registers, and program counters.

CFB   Cipher feedback.

Channel   Communication channel such as wire, fiber optics, air, or free space through which information flows.

Checksum   Block of parity checks or similar computations that are derived with dependence on every bit.

Chip   Small piece of semiconductor substrate (usually containing an integrated circuit.

Cipher block chaining (CBC)   Entire block of ciphertext is exclusive-ored with the plaintext.

Cipher feedback mode (CFB)   Passing ciphertext through a nonlinear block cipher to derive key characters.

Ciphertext   Text that has been encoded to protect the information from unauthorized observation.

Circuit breaker   Magnetic or electromechanical device that self-interrupts when power demands become excessive.

Cladding   Material surrounding fiber-optic cable core intended to refract energy along the core.

Clarke orbit   A geosynchronous orbit.

Class A fire   Fire of ordinary combustibles (such as paper, wood, cloth, or plastics).

Class B fire   Flammable liquid and vapor fire.

Class C fire   Fires involving electrical energy.

Classified data Data requiring protection against unauthorized disclosure in the interest of national security.

Cleartext Ordinary text as it would be transmitted uncoded.

Clock A signal occurring at regular intervals from which to derive system timing.

Coaxial cable Transmission energy confined between an outer cylindrical shield and an inner conductor.

Code Depending on the context, either a digital representation of numbers, letters, or symbols; or a program.

Code book A listing of plaintext items and equivalent code segments.

Codebreaking Deciphering a cryptogram without the key by an unintended recipient.

Codec Coder-decoder term for a device that codes analog signals (such as video or voice) onto carrier modulation that can be transmitted over such communication media as twisted pairs, phone lines, coax, fiber optics, and electromagnetic energy.

Coding A method for representing information in a different form (for example, ASCII representation of alphanumeric characters, BCD representation of numbers, or programming statements for instructions). None of these methods provide cryptographic protection because they are always done the same way, which is either immediately obvious or can be eventually deduced or discovered. Coding is not normally used for security.

Cold site A backup or recovery facility into which computers can be moved by members in case of a disaster (a shell).

Combinational logic Circuit for mapping digital inputs to a digital output or outputs. Combinational logic consists of gates and inverters and has no memory.

Common-mode noise Noise appearing on both sides of the transmitting conductor pair.

Communications engineer A staff member who works with the communications equipment that convey computer data. Such equipment might include wiring, modems, encryption equipment, diagnostic and monitoring equipment.

Compiler language Higher-order language approximating the programmer's common usage. FORTRAN, ALGOL, and PASCAL are examples of compiler languages.

Complement Changing 1 to 0 and 0 to 1.

Computer Relatively high-speed device containing a CPU to execute instructions, memory, I/O, and software.

Computer operator Person in control of basic computer operations, usually from a console.

Computer-security specialist   Person responsible for planning, implementation, installation, operation, and evaluation of security safeguards and controls.

Computer-systems engineer   Person responsible for system (CPU and peripheral) hardware, including test, diagnosis, and repair.

Concentrator ("multiplexer")   A device that connects several input lines sequentially to a single output line so that the output carries interspersed data from several sources.

Confidentiality   Status requiring protection from unauthorized disclosure.

Contingency plan   Procedures for emergency response, backup, and recovery in the event of disaster.

Contingency planning   Program to minimize the potential disruption of computing capabilities in case of a disaster.

Controller   A dedicated processor that controls some activity or process that cannot be used for general purposes.

Core   Small magnetic toroid used in computer memories.

COS   A Cray Systems Inc. operating system intended primarily for batch processing.

Cross-talk   Coupling of energy from one circuit or wire to another.

CRT (cathode ray tube)   A display device.

Cryptogram   The ciphertext.

Cryptography   A method of rendering information unintelligible by transformation.

Cryptosystem   A system that encrypts and decrypts information.

CSMA (carrier sense multiple access)   Access attempts depend upon sensing no carrier from other sources already on the line.

CVSD   Continuously variable slope delta modulation.

Cyclic redundancy check (CRC) codes   A family of error-correcting codes depending on linear polynomial algebra.

DAA   Data authentication algorithm.

DAC   Data authentication code.

Daisy chaining   Succession or chain of I/O ports connected by combinational logic that pass a signal along the chain until the first active source is detected and that block detection of subsequent active sources until the first active source has been acknowledged.

Database   A collection of data organized so it can be searched according to characteristics of the data.

Database administrator   A system or person adding, modifying, or deleting records in on-line and off-line database systems.

Data diddling   Altering data before computer input.

Data Encryption Standard (DES)   An encryption algorithm for coding binary data blocks or bit streams by a sequence of permutations and algebraic operations. The technique has been approved and is supported analytically by the National Bureau of Standards.

DATAPAC   Trans-Canada Telephone System offering packet switched service.

Data-security officer (DSO)   The person responsible for protecting data processing systems and for protecting against data misuse.

Data terminal   Device typically containing a teletype keyboard, telephone line modem, and cassette tape memory. A data terminal is used to communicate with computer time-share networks and processor-based systems.

DBMS   Database management system.

DDD (Direct Distance Dial)   Nationwide long-distance network allowing long-distance calls without operator intervention.

DDN   Defense Digital Network.

DDP   Distributed data processing.

DDS   Dataphone Digital Service.

Deciphering   Translating ciphertext to cleartext (usually by utilizing a key).

Degausser   A magnetic-field generating device used to remove information from magnetic media such as tapes and disks. The device generates an alternating field; by placing the source near the magnetic media the stored DC field patterns are overridden.

Demultiplexer   Circuit that electronically switches an input to one of several outputs.

DES (Data Encryption Standard)   A standard issued by the U.S. Bureau of Standards as an approved technique for encoding nonclassified sensitive digital information.

Descendant   A node in a tree structure derived from or subservient to another node.

Dibit PSK (dibit-phase shift-keying)   A technique for modulating information onto a carrier by shifting the carrier phase according to each pair of bits processed.

Die, dice   Sometimes used to describe chips (integrated circuit on a piece of semiconductor material).

Digital   Discretely variable.

Digital data   Data represented by digits in a number base or code system.

Digital loopback   Diagnostic technique by connecting digital output of receiving modem to digital input and looping back to transmitting modem.

Directory   Descriptive information pertaining to files and file-access controls.

Discretionary-access controls   Access controls that can be specified by a user to entities owned by the user.

Disk   Magnetic recording device for mass storage using a flat, circular recording medium.

Diskette   Thin, circular flexible sheet of Mylar with a magnetic-oxide surface on which data can be recorded in tracks and from which data can be read. Sometimes called a floppy disk.

Distributed processing A system including linked CPUs in which processing takes place in more than one CPU.

Distributed systems Systems whose components are not centrally located and are connected by communication media.

DLE Data-line escape.

DM (delta modulation) Pulse code information representing the direction of change since the last data rather than any absolute value of information or amount of charge.

Downlink Transmission link from a satellite to an earth station.

DP Data processing (usually by computers).

DPCM Differential pulse code modulation, using a two-digit code to represent various prescribed changes that can occur in the data.

DPDT Double-pole, double-throw switch configuration.

DTE Data terminal equipment.

Duplex Simultaneous bidirectional data transmission (by multiplexing or separate lines).

Duplex channel A channel through which information can flow in both directions.

ECCM Electronic counter-countermeasures.

ECM Electronic countermeasures.

EDP Electronic-data processing.

EDP auditor A person who performs an independent security analysis and performance check of computer systems by reviewing and testing performance and security features.

EIA Electronic Industries Association, which formulates interface standards.

EIRP (effective isotropic-radiated power) Contour lines on a map showing relative power delivered as a function of geographic location.

Electromagnetic energy Energy conveyed by the propagation of electric fields and magnetic fields, oscillating in a direction transverse to the direction of propagation.

Electronic mail A technique for conveying messages from one station of the system to other designated stations electronically. A computer is usually used to store and retrieve messages on demand when stations wish to examine their mail. Usually includes such features as labeling capabilities for maintaining files, editing capabilities, and requests for acknowledgment.

Emergency response Immediate action taken in the event of a disaster to limit overall effects and computing impact.

EMI Electromagnetic interference.

EMT (electrical metallic tubing)   Conduit that provides some physical and electrical protection for wiring.

Encipher   Transform plain text to ensure communication privacy.

Encryption   Encoding information so that it cannot be deciphered without the encryption key.

EOT   End of transmission.

Ergonomics   Work efficiency techniques.

Error correcting/detecting codes   Codes that use redundant information to the data transmitted to detect or the correct certain types of errors made during the transmission process.

ET   Earth terminal.

Ethernet   A local network communication system operating on baseband with bus contention and packet transmission, supported and developed by Xerox, Intel, and DEC.

ETX   End of text.

Eutectic metal   Metal with a very low melting point temperature used as a mechanical fuse.

Exclusive-OR (XOR)   An operation where two bits of data are operated on, giving a result of 1 if the bit operands are different and 0 if the bit operands are the same.

Faraday shield   A screen or cage of wires intended to protect against the transmission of electrostatic energy.

Facsimile   An image digitized and transmitted as digital data.

FCC (Federal Communications Commission)   A U.S. regulatory body responsible for interstate communication and common carrier services.

FDM (frequency-division multiplexing)   A strategy for connecting multiple input sources to a single output by converting the inputs to different frequencies, which can be carried simultaneously on the output medium.

FDMA   Frequency-division multiple access.

FEC (forward error correction)   The capability within the information transmitted to self-correct certain types of errors.

Fiber optics   Glass fibers for modulated light wave transmission.

FIFO   First-in, first-out memory technique (buffer).

FIPS Pubs   Federal Information Processing Standards Publications.

Floppy disk   Low-cost mass storage medium usually consisting of a thin, circular flexible sheet of Mylar with a magnetic-oxide surface on which data can be recorded in tracks and from which data can be read. Sometimes called a diskette.

Firmware   A piece of hardware (for example, a ROM) that implements a software routine.

Footprint   Term for satellite coverage, measured in terms of EIRP (contours of constant power).

FSK (frequency shift keying) A technique for modulating information onto a carrier.

Fiber optics The conveyance of energy in the optical frequency band through very small fibers of material that are transparent to optical frequency radiation.

Fire walls Walls that have been sufficiently fireproofed to prevent the spread of fires.

Fixed-length cipher A replacement is made for each letter or group of letters.

Frequency agile Capable of varying frequencies over a substantial range.

Full duplex Transmission both directions simultaneously.

Group access Common (shared) file access for a group of users.

Half duplex A channel that can carry information in either direction, but not at the same time.

Halogen Chemical series including fluorine, chlorine, bromine and iodine.

Halon system A fire suppression system using Halon gas. Halon is especially suited for computer facilities because it does not damage electronic equipment or harm humans.

Handshaking An interchange of signals between two devices that must communicate to prepare for or terminate a connection or data transfer.

Hardware Circuit components and associated equipment.

HDLC High-level data-link control (full duplex).

Hierarchy Ordering of importance, ranking, or sequencing.

High-level language Powerful user-oriented language such as a compiler language or a highly capable interpreter.

Hollerith code Format for data punching on IBM (and other) computer cards.

Host A computer that accepts and processes jobs from remote terminals or computers.

Hot site A backup or recovery computer facility that can be temporarily used by members in case of a disaster.

Index of refraction Property of materials indicating the wavelength of electromagnetic energy relative to the corresponding wavelength in free space.

Integrity Protection against accidental or intentional destruction or modification.

Intelligent terminal A data communications terminal with data storage and processing capabilities.

Intelligent typewriters Typewriters with memory and logic built in to allow minor editing.

Interactive Real-time dialogue between terminal and computer.

Interoffice trunks Connections between telephone company central offices.

Interpretive language High-order language similar to compiler language, but each statement is individually converted to machine language.

Intertoll trunks Telephone company term for connection between toll offices.

ISDN (Integrated Services Digital Network) A digital communications network that can handle multiple services (such as data, voice, video, or facsimile).

ISO (Internatinal Standards Organization) An international body for establishing communications standards.

Isochronous Intermediate between synchronous and asynchronous utilizing transitional encoding to link data to a clock rate higher than the data rate with possible pulse stuffing.

ISO protocol A layered set of standards for data communication proposed by the International Standards Organization.

IV (initialization vector) IV is used as a starting point for an encryption process.

Jamming The intentional insertion of a signal or noise into a system (usually electromagnetically) to prevent normal operation of the system.

JCL (job control language) An IBM-supported software utility.

Journaling Logging significant events and providing accountability.

K Symbol for 1,024.

Kbps Thousands of bits per second.

Kernelized operating systems Systems designed to partition the users so that they cannot gain access to parts of the system for which they are not authorized. Such systems appear to users as if there were completely different computers available to users of different kernels or classes. Systems can be kernelized by hardware or software techniques (or both).

Key (1) Physical entity to unlock and sometimes lock a lock; (2) an electronic signal or data pattern to allow the logical operation desired; (3) a combination of characters, numbers, or both to be examined prior to granting access to a physical area or to a computer, or to a file of data.

Key generator A device for encrypting-key generation.

Key loader A self-contained device that can be attached to encryption equipment for loading an encryption key.

Key notarization A technique for encrypting information at a terminal site before transmission to a host computer over communication media that might be vulnerable to interception. The system depends on the ability of the host and the terminal to maintain the same encryption key and algorithm. It is often accomplished by "downloading" (sending information) from the host to the terminal on key changes. This downloaded information must also be encrypted.

KG (key generator) An encryption device.

Knapsack A problem used in encryption that is difficult to solve without key information, but easy to solve with the information.

Knapsack cipher An algorithmic solution of a function of operands manipulated so that the solution is relatively easy for the recipient who has furnished the keys, but relatively difficult for a person not in possession of the keys.

KSOS A kernelized operating system.

LAN Local area networks.

Language Method for communicating with a processor by entering symbols (for example, numbers, alphabetic characters, or mathematical operators) into the system. Variations range from machine-oriented languages (sequences of bit patterns) to people-oriented languages (words and equations).

LC Looped clock.

Library Collection of software programs or routines.

LIFO Last-in, first-out memory consisting of a series of registers acting as a stack. A word read from LIFO must be the last word written to the LIFO. LIFOs are sometimes called push-down stacks or push-pop stacks.

Linear Operation where superposition holds—specifically, mathematics based on linear algebra (such as groups, fields, rings, vector spaces).

Link A connection (not necessarily hardwired) for communication.

Loader Software program for loading a program into memory.

Local loop Telephone company term for connection between the telephone and the local central office.

Local networks (local area networks) Interconnection and communication mechanisms for office and computer-data traffic that allows common access to a communication medium. The usual distances spanned are on the order of a mile or less.

Logic bombs Unauthorized, malicious destructive routines that are initiated by some parameter such as time and date.

Logic operations Operations usually on binary numbers that are analogous to thought processes and that are readily realized by circuitry. These operations are the basis for computer design.

LOS Line of sight.

MACS Multiline automatic-calling system.

Magnetic core Small doughnut-shaped devices that retain permanent magnetic flux either clockwise or counterclockwise. These device are often used in large-scale computer memory systems.

Mainframe computers Large central-site computers that provide state-of-the-art computing capabilities.

Mbps Millions of bits per second.

MDC Modification detection code.

MDEA Modification detection encryption algorithm.

Memory Computer accessible storage area for information and data.

Mean time before failure (MTBF) Measure of system reliability.

Mesh network A network interconnection topology that gives the capability for almost all nodes to communicate with all other nodes.

Microcomputer A small computer based on a microprocessor and intended for individual use.

Microcontroller Depending on the context, used as either a microprocessor-based logic system dedicated to exercising some sort of system control or a microprogrammed control system.

Microprocessor A small device usually built on a small semiconductor chip that has rudimentary computer capabilities (such as instruction processing, logic, arithmetic, and control).

Microwave link An electromagnetic communication channel from antenna to antenna through the air at frequencies ranging from thousands of Hertz (cycles per second) to billions of Hertz.

Minicomputer A small (usually desk size) computer with relatively limited capabilities, compared to mainframes.

Modem (modulator-demodulator) A device that receives digital data (alphanumeric characters or commands) and conveys the information by modulating a carrier for transmission over such communication media as twisted pairs, coax, fiber optics, phone lines, or via electromagnetic energy.

Modulation The process of introducing variations into a carrier to convey intelligence.

Modulo algebra A mathematical system with a finite number of symbols and a counting system structured like a ring so that the first symbol sequences immediately following the last.

Modulo-2 addition Exclusive-OR addition, where an even number of input ones results in a zero output, and an odd number of input ones results in a one output.

MULTICS A kernelized operating system.

Multidrops Multiple attachments to a bus communication system.

Multiplexer (or concentrator) A device that sequentially connects several input lines to a single output line so that the output carries interspersed data from several sources.

Multiplexing Interleaving or simultaneously transmitting two or more messages on a single channel.

MVS An IBM operating system.

NBS   National Bureau of Standards.

Network security controller   A computer that validates security privileges (such as passwords, file access, and use restrictions) for a network of computing devices. For security reasons, the network security controller runs no user code.

Networks   Associated components interconnected for such functions as communications and resource sharing.

NFPA   National Fire Protection Association.

Node   A network termination point (computer, terminal, switch).

Nonvolatile memory   Memory that is retained when power is shut off.

NOS   A Control Data Corporation operating system primarily for interactive processing.

NP problem   A problem that has no known solution in practical time (nondeterministic polynomial time problem).

NRZ   Nonreturn to zero.

NSA   National Security Agency.

NSC   Network security controller or center.

Object code   The representation of a program after translation from source code to a form directly executable by a computer.

OCR   Optical character reader.

OEM (original equipment manufacturer)   Usually, a company that incorporates products from suppliers into an original product and markets the product under its own name.

Office automation   A term for an electronic station or network of stations that allow functions like electronic filing, electronic mail, meeting and other scheduling reminders, word processing, and computing to be carried out through a computer or a network of computers.

Office workstations   Equipment located on a desk or at a work station that allows automated assistance with office work.

One-way cipher (one-way encryption)   An irreversible function (transformation) from plaintext to ciphertext.

Operating system   The software furnished by a manufacturer for a computer system to control its mode of operation and interface with users.

PABX (private automated branch exchange)   Local telephone or data control switch.

Packet switching   The logical message-transmission strategy of segmenting messages into relatively short portions (packets) so that each packet can be routed efficiently through the network according to the network status at the time the packet enters the network.

Parity   A measure of the number of ones in a sequence; either odd or even.

Passphrase   A phrase used in the same manner as a password to control user access.

Password   A protected word or string of characters for user authentication or verification of access authorization.

PBX (Private Branch Exchange)   A central switching center of the type used by the telephone companies.

PCM (pulse code modulation)   A strategy for coding data by using pulses of voltage.

Personal computers   Computers originally intended for use in the home by hobbyists or for operations not related to business. These are now commonly used as small business computers.

Phase jitter   Uncertainty in phase position due to transmission and equipment variations.

PIN (personal identification number)   A user's private code for entry into access-control systems like ATMs. Also a common photodetection diode using p type, intrinsic type and n type semiconductor material.

Plaintext   Text that appears in memory coded only by whatever means are necessary for electronic transmission with no encryption coding being used.

Polling   Sequential sampling or reading information that has been stored awaiting a query.

Port   Connection through which information can pass interfacing one system with another.

Port contender   A device that allows connection from a relatively large number of inputs to a relatively small number of output ports, usually on a first-come first-served basis, with queuing.

Power factor   Ratio of actual to potential power.

Power-line disturbance analyzer   An instrument for identifying and characterizing various power problems.

PPM   (1) pulse-position modulation; (2) parts per million.

Prime number   An integer that cannot be evenly divided by another integer greater than one.

Privacy   Right (legal or social) of an individual to control collection, storing and dissemination of personal information.

Processor   Device for interpreting and acting on program inputs.

Product cipher   A composition of encryptions.

Programmed   (1) controlled by software; (2) controlled by hardware or firmware (hardware) implementation of software.

Programming   Depending on the context have various meanings including (1) writing a sequence of instructions; (2) physically inserting data into ROM or PROM; or (3) setting up an address by electrical connections to which particular devices (memory elements or input/output devices) will respond.

Protocol   Rules, procedures, or format for presenting information sequentially.

Public key cryptosystem   The encryption process depends on using the recipient's public key; the decryption by the recipient depends on the use of the recipient's private key.

Pulse stuffing   Buffered handling of pulses so that pulses are added artificially to prevent underflow (more reads from buffer than writes to buffer).

PSK (phase shift keying)   A technique for modulating information onto a carrier by shifting the carrier phase.

PSOS (Provably Secure Operating System)

PSTN   Public switched telephone network.

Queue   A "waiting area" of memory for temporary storage, or buffering.

RAM (random-access memory)   A read-write memory that data can be written into as well as read out from.

Random access   Memory access to a specified location without waiting to arrive at the data or data location sequentially.

Read   Process of examining data in memory by deriving signals that directly represent the data. Reading is usually a nondestructive process. That is, the data are unaltered in memory after the read process.

Recovery   Restoration of computing facilities and capabilities.

Red/black concept   Separation and routing control to prevent inadvertent coupling between red (carrying classified) and black (not protected for classified) wiring.

Register   Storage device for temporarily storing a group of associated bits.

Regulator   A system that automatically maintains a specific characteristic (such as voltage, current, power, speed, or frequency).

Releases   Supported modifications made to languages, operating systems, and other software.

Remote terminal   A terminal located away from the central site.

Removable storage media   Tapes, disk packs, or floppy diskettes that can be easily removed from the system.

Rf   Radio frequency (generally high kHz to MHz range).

RFI   Radio frequency interference.

Ringer isolators   Devices that can be inserted in a telephone ringer circuit to filter out energy that might have been coupled to the circuit from nearby radiating sources. These devices isolate the radiating sources from the telephone circuits.

Ring network   A network interconnection topology that involves sequential node connection so that communication takes place around a ring (clockwise or counterclockwise).

Risk analysis   A technique for quantifying the value of statistically expected losses resulting from vulnerabilities and for quantifying the cost per unit of time of techniques for combating the vulnerabilities. The resulting cost comparisons help in evaluating the desirability of the security measures.

RJE (remote job-entry station)   A hardware station at which jobs can be submitted to a computer system.

RJET (remote job-entry terminal)   A remote pheripheral processor that controls communication between remotely located users and a central computer.

ROM (read-only memory)   Memory from which data can be obtained and in which the data are permanently fixed according to specification when ordering the part.

RSA encryption   A public-key cryptosystem that provides capabilities for secrecy and authentication. Named for Rivest, Shamir, and Adelman.

RS 232   A standard communication protocol and physical (connectors and wire usage) standard often used to interconnect terminals and modems.

Running key cipher   A cipher for which the key length is the same as the message length.

Salami technique   The process of removing small slices of assets so that removal is unnoticed but aggregate over time is substantial.

Sanitizing   Erasing or overwriting information so it will not be inadvertently disclosed.

Satellite   Object orbiting around the earth.

S-box   A nonlinear function used in the DES algorithm.

Scavenging   Physical or electronic search for remnant data that may have not been properly destroyed (such as reading assigned file space prior to writing into the space).

SCR (silicon-controlled rectifier)   A device that can be triggered into conduction by a control voltage.

Scrambler   A device used to rearrange a sequence of symbols or frequencies, usually for balancing considerations. Scrambling achieves rudimentary coding, but it is inferior to encryption because theoretically the scrambling pattern cannot be protected indefinitely.

Scrambling   Mixing up the order of data in a prescribed way.

Security   Protection from harm, such as unintended disclosure, alteration, destruction, misuse, or vandalism.

Security kernel   Central hardware or software that performs security functions.

Security specialist   A person responsible for planning, implementing, installing, and monitoring security safeguards and controls.

Separation of duties   The concept of dichotomizing at least some of the functions of authorizing, approving, recording, issuing, paying, reviewing, auditing, programming, and developing operating systems among separate personnel.

Session key A common key shared between a transmitter and a receiver during a data-processing session involving encrypted text.

Shell A backup or recovery facility (a cold site) into which computers can be moved in case of a disaster.

Shielded cable Coaxial cable with the transmission energy confined between an outer cylindrical shield and a central conductor.

Slaved synchronous Source and sync use the same clock.

Slotted ALOHA A broadcast technique similar to ALOHA (users can broadcast at almost any time); however, broadcast times must start at the beginning of specific time slot intervals.

Smoke detector Device that senses particles of combustion.

SOH Start of heading.

Software Programs of instructions, including the operating programs and programs for editing, program conversion, and loading data into memory.

Source code The representation of a program as written by a programmer or as otherwise entered into the initial computer processing.

Spoofing Unauthorized insertion, modification, or deletion of information.

Standalone A system that functions independently of other systems.

Star network A network-interconnection topology built around a central control point that communicates with the peripheral nodes of the network.

STAT MUX Statistical multiplexer.

Statistical multiplexer A multiplexer with logic to apportion channel capacity to the most active users without being constrained to predetermined rules for allocation.

Steganography A method of concealing the existence of information.

Store and forward Message storage at an intermediate location before subsequent transmission.

Stream cipher Each character or bit is enciphered with an individual element of the key. A periodic stream cipher repeats regularly; a synchronous stream cipher has a key stream independent of the message stream so that the transmitter and the receiver must be synchronized; and a self-synchronous stream cipher has key characters derived from previously transmitted cipher text.

STX Start of text.

Subcarrier A signal piggybacked on the main signal to convey additional information.

Subkey A key to allow access to a subset of a database.

Superminicomputers Advanced minicomputers with many of the capabilities formerly found only in mainframes.

Superzapping   A utility program that bypasses protective controls and is used in an emergency by system operators to delete information.

Symmetric cryptosystem   A system that uses the same key for encryption and decryption.

SYN   Sync character.

Synchronous   System operation keyed to a common clock.

System software   Programs that extend system capabilities.

Systems programmer   Software developer responsible for design, development, installation, and documentation of the operating system, peripheral utility programs, and modifications.

TADI   Time assignment data interpolation (data inserted in idle voice periods).

Tape librarian   Person in charge of filing, retrieving, and accounting for storage media (tapes, disk packs, cartridges).

TASI   Time assignment speech interpolation.

TDM (time-division multiplexing)   Sharing of an output line by several input lines with sequential connection of inputs to the output.

TDMA/DA (time-division multiple-access demand assignment)   A multiplexing technique that is varied dynamically according to user requirements.

Telecommunications   Communication over relatively large (usually more than a few hundred meters) distances, usually by microwave, but sometimes over hardwired lines.

Telenet (GTE-Telenet)   Commercial packet-switched network.

Telephone tag   The process that occurs when a caller fails to reach intended party but leaves a message to return the call; the return call finds the original caller unavailable, so the return caller leaves a message; etc.

Teleprocessing   Data processing over telecommunication links.

Teletext   Electronically conveyed printed material, usually using the vertical blanking interval in a television sweep.

TELEX   Western Union exchange-switching service for teleprinters.

Tempest   A term commonly used to describe for the emanation of information by unintended means such as electromagnetic, electrical, and acoustic propagation so that it might be intercepted by unauthorized persons.

Terminal   A data-entry device for communicating alphanumeric characters, programs, and commands to computers and similar devices. They may or may not have "intelligence" (the ability to store, modify, or edit data before transmission).

Terminal masquerade problem   An attack where the user of a terminal communicates with another system terminal in such a way that the system thinks communication is coming from a different terminal than it really is.

Thermocouple A device that delivers increased voltage in response to increased temperature.

Tiger teams Teams of experts who try to penetrate the security features of a computer system as a test of its robustness.

Toll-connecting trunk Connection between telephone company central office and toll office.

Topology Structure of network interconnection.

Transparent Internal actions that are not obvious to external users.

Transponder A receiver/transmitter relay device that repeats the received signal for retransmission with amplification.

Trap doors (1) breaks in programs to allow for insertion of steps and to provide intermediate output for diagnosis; and (2) cryptographic techniques for solving a computationally difficult problem by using additional crucial information.

Tree A graphic representation of a mathematic structure with a starting point (root), nodes that are direct descendants of other nodes, and leaves that have no descendants.

Trojan horse Covert unauthorized instruction sequence within an authorized program.

Trunks Shared communication links between nodes or switches.

Turing machine (TM) A finite-state machine model with an infinite read/write tape.

Turnkey An integrated piece of equipment installed and ready to use.

Twisted pairs A pair of wires that are twisted together to minimize capacitance and radiated energy.

TWX Teletypewriter exchange service provided by Western Union.

Tymnet Commercial packet-switched network.

UART Universal asynchronous receiver/transmitter.

Uninterruptible Power Supply (UPS) A system that can maintain AC power during a temporary outage by continuing to derive DC power from batteries and convert to AC power in the event that commercial power becomes unavailable or outside normal limits. Usually, such systems also include filtering, regulating, and other power conditioning for delivered power whether derived from the internal or the external supply.

UNIX A Bell Laboratories–designed operating system.

UPC (Universal Product Code) Product-label code containing data that can be converted by the system to price.

Uplink Transmission link from an earth station to a satellite.

User-friendly A system or program that is easy for users to learn; usually developed for nonprofessionals.

User programmer A person who designs, develops, tests, documents, and maintains programs in accordance with user-determined specifications (if any).

Variable length code A replacement symbol (any length) is used for each plaintext symbol.

VF Voice frequency.

Virtual circuit A logical connection established ad hoc and is transparent to the connection terminations.

Volatile memory Memory that is lost when power is removed.

Vulnerability assessment A review of the susceptibility of a system or program to loss or unauthorized use.

WATS (wide-area telephone service) A long-distance telephone service contracted for on a high-volume bulk basis instead of on the basis of individual calls.

Weigand effect Ferromagnetic wire magnetization effect.

Wiretapping Passive monitoring of communication channel surreptitiously.

Word Group of associated digits.

Word processor A text-preparation device that contains memory and intelligence so that text material can be edited electronically before printing.

Write Process of inserting data into memory. This process is destructive, in that any data already in a particular memory location are destroyed when new data are written into that location.

Write ring A ring that can be inserted into a reel of magnetic tape that enables the tape-deck writing process. Removal of the write ring prevents writing.

X.25 protocol Synchronous international serial interface standard used in public packet-switched networks.

X.28 Asynchronous international serial interface standard.

References

Aho, A.V., and J.D. Ullman, *Principles of Compiler Design* (Reading, Mass.: Addison-Wesley, 1979).

Allen, Brandt, "Threat Teams: A Technique for Detection and Prevention of Fraud in Automated and Manual Systems," *Computer Security Journal,* Spring 1981.

Anderson, James P., "Systems Architecture for Security and Protection," *NBS Special Publication 404,* March 1974.

Asimov, Isaac, "The Electronic Mail," *American Way,* April 1983.

Austin, Brian B., "Controlling Physical Access from a Central Location," *Computer Security Journal,* Spring 1981.

Backwith, Nigel, "Unique Approach to Security Evaluation," *Computers and Security,* January 1983.

Ball, Leslie D., and others, "Disaster Recovery Services," *Computers and Security,* vol. 1, no. 3, November 1982.

Banerjee, Subokh K., "High Speed Implementation of DES," *Computers and Security,* November 1982.

Battelle-Northwest, Pacific Northwest Lab., "Pacific Northwest Laboratory ADP Risk Assessment Document—Computer Hardware," *Battelle Form A-1004-125,* March 1983.

———— "Pacific Northwest Laboratory ADP Risk Assessment Document—Software Applications," *Battelle Form A-1004-124,* March 1983.

Beeler, Jeffry, "Destroyed Data Center Up a Week Later," *Computerworld,* March 21, 1983.

Beitman, Lawrence, "Practical Guide to Small Business Computer Security," *The Office,* August 1982.

Benice, Daniel D., *Introduction to Computers and Data Processing* (Englewood Cliffs, N.J.: Prentice Hall, 1970).

Benjamin, Robert, "Local Area Networks: The Legend of the Ring, The Star and the Tree," *Office Products News,* September 1981.

Bequai, A., *Computer Crime* (Lexington, Mass.: Lexington Books, 1978).

Bodson, Dennis, "EMP, Lightning and Power Transients: Their Threat and Relevance to EMP Protection Standards for Telecommunication Facilities," National Communications System Technology and Standards *NCS-TIB-78-1,* August 1978.

Brickell, E.F., J.A. Davis, and G.J. Simmons, "A Preliminary Report on the Cryptoanalysis of Merkle-Hellman Knapsack Cryptosystems," paper presented at Crypto '82, Santa Barbara, Calif., August 1982. *Advances in Cryptology* (New York, NY: Plenum Press, 1983).

—— and G.J. Simmons, "A Status Report on Knapsack-Based Public Key Cryptosystems," Sandia Laboratories *SAND 83-0042,* February 1983.

Budginski, Robert, "Single-Chip Computer Scrambles for Security," *Electronics,* July 19, 1979.

Caprigno, Richard, and Gurcharn S. Dang, "Specifying Uninterruptible Power Systems," *Digital Design,* March 1983.

Cerullo, Michael J., "Data Communications Controls," *Computers and Security,* January 1983.

Chadwick, H.A., "Burning Down the Data Center," *Datamation,* October 1975.

Clark, George C., Jr., and J. Bibb Cain, *Error Correction Coding for Digital Communications* (New York, N.Y.: Plenum Press, 1981).

Computer Security Institute, *1980 Computer Security Buyers' Guide* (Northborough, Mass.: CSI Press, 1979).

——, *Computer Security Manual* (Northborough, Mass.: CSI Press, 1980).

Cooper, James Arlin, *Microprocessor Background for Management Personnel* (Englewood Cliffs, N.J.: Prentice-Hall, 1981).

Corynen, G.C., "A Methodology for Assessing the Security Risks Associated with Computer Sites and Networks, Part 1," Lawrence Livermore National Laboratory, June 23, 1982.

Cuccia, C. Loins, "Satellite Communications and the Information Decade," *Microwave Journal,* January 1982.

Cunningham, D. Jay, "The Impact of Fiber Optics on Local Area Networks," *Telephony,* January 3, 1983.

Data Communications, A User's Handbook (Sunnyvale, CA.: Racal-Vadic Corporation, undated).

"Data Security in Computer Networks," *Computer,* February 1983.

Davidson, Malcolm, "Understanding the High Speed Digital Logic Signal," *Computer Design,* November 1982.

Davies, Donald W. "Tutorial: The Security of Data in Networks" Institute of Electrical and Electronics, Inc., cat. no. EH0183-4, 1982.

Denning, Dorothy Elizabeth Robling, *Cryptography and Data Security* (Reading, Mass.: Addison-Wesley, 1982).

Diffie, Whitfield, and Martin E. Hellman, "Exhaustive Cryptanalysis of the NBS Data Encryption Standard," *Computer,* June 1977.

——, "New Directions in Cryptography," *IEEE Transactions on Information Theory,* vol. IT-22(6), November 1976.

Doddington, G.R., "Personal Identity Verification Using Voice," paper presented at Electro 1976 Conference, May 1976.

Easton, Anthony T., *The Home Satellite TV Book* (New York, N.Y.: Wideview Books, 1982).

EDP Audit Control's Inc., "Computer Network Security in DOE Installations," report prepared for the Sandia National Laboratories, January 1981.

Ehrsam, W.F., S.M. Matyas, C.H. Meyer, and W.L. Tuckman, "A Cryptographic Key Management Scheme for Implementing the Data Encryption Standard," *IBM System Journal,* vol. 11, no. 2, 1978.

Eleccion, Marce, "Automatic Fingerprint Identification," *IEEE Spectrum,* September 1973.

Friedman, S.D., "Contingency and Disaster Planning," *Computers and Security,* January 1982.

Gaade, R.P.R., "Picking Up the Pieces," *Datamation,* January 1980.

Gear, C. William, *Computer Organization and Programming* (New York: McGraw-Hill, 1969).

Gifford, David K., "Cryptographic Sealing for Information and Authentication," *Communications of the ACM,* April 1982.

Glazer, Sarah, "Communicating by Satellite: Options for Small Computers," *Mini-Micro Systems,* March 1983.

Goldstein, R.C., *The Cost of Privacy* (Brighton, Me.: Honeywell Information Systems, 1975).

Goldstein, Robert, "The Cost of Computer Privacy and Security," *Proceedings of Computer Security and Privacy Symposium,* April 1975.

Grant, Peter, "Shielding Techniques Tackle EMI Excesses," *Microwaves,* October 1982.

Grunelle, Robert, "Meeting the New Radio Interference Standards," *Digital Design,* November 1982.

Held, Gilbert, "Locking Intruders Out of a Network," *Data Communications,* January/February 1975.

Herbst, N.M., and C.N. Liu, "Automatic Signature Verification Based on Accuracy," *IBM Journal of Research and Development,* May 1977.

Hill, Frederick J., and Gerald R. Peterson, *Digital Systems: Hardware Organization and Design, 2nd ed. (New York: Wiley, 1978).*

Hindon, Harvey J., *"LSI-Based Data Encryption Discourages the Data Thief,"* Electronics, June 21, 1979.

Hoffman, L.J. *Security and Privacy in Computer Systems* (Los Angeles, CA.: Melville Publishing, 1973).

Hsiao, David K., Douglass S. Kerr, and Stuart E. Madnick, *Computer Security* (New York: Academic Press, 1979).

Humphrey, Thomas, and Frank Toth, "Two-Chip Data Encryption Unit Supports Multi-Key Systems," *Electronics,* January 17, 1980.

Huntsman, James, "Proper Shielding Protects ICs from Electrostatic Damage," *Electronics,* July 14, 1982.

Johnston, Robert E., "Security Software Packages—A Question and Answer Comparison of the 'Big 3,' " *Computer Security Journal,* Spring 1981.

Kahn, D., *Codebreakers* (New York: Macmillan, 1967).

Keck, Donald B., "Single-Mode Fibers Outperform Multimode Cables," *IEEE Spectrum,* March 1983.

Keiser, Bernhard E., "Digital Modulation Techniques Compared," *Microwaves and RF,* April 1983.

Kelleher, Joanne, "Computer Security: A Double Threat," *Business Computer Systems,* October 1982.

Key, A.A., and J.A. Cooper, "Central Computing Facility (CCF) Password Management: A Status Report," Sandia National Laboratories *SAND 81-0467,* March 1981.

Kiu, C.N., N.M. Herbst, and M.J. Anthony, "Automatic Signature Verification: System Description and Field Test Results," *IEEE Transactions: Systems, Man, and Cybernetics,* January 1979.

Kolata, Gena, "Partners in Crime: Ripoff Artists and Computers," *Smithsonian,* August 1982.

Konheim, Alan G., *Cryptography: A Primer* (New York: Wiley, 1981).

Koningsford, W.L., "Developing Standards for Operating System Security," *Computer Security Journal,* Spring 1981.

Kraus, Leonard J., and Aileen MacGahan, *Computer Fraud and Countermeasures* (Englewood Cliffs, N.J.: Prentice-Hall, 1979).

Kressign, Gerald, "A Model to Describe Protection Problems," *Proceedings* of the 1980 Symposium on Security and Privacy, Oakland, Calif., April 14–16, 1980.

Kuck, David J., *The Structure of Computers and Computations,* vol. 1 (New York: Wiley, 1978).

Kunz, Heinrich, "Electrostatic Charging and Simulation of the Discharging Process," *EMC Technology,* April 1982.

Landwehr, Carl, "Protecting Stored Data Remains a Serious Problem," *Military Electronics/Countermeasures,* April 1983.

Lempel, A., "Cryptography in Transition: A Survey," *Computer Survey,* vol. 11, no. 4, December 1979.

McCauley, E., and others, "KSOS—The Design of a Secure Operating System," paper presented at the AFIPS National Computer Conference, 1979.

McGlynn, Daniel R., *Distributed Processing and Data Communications* (New York: Wiley, 1978).

MacMillan, D., "Single Chip Encrypts Data at 14 MB/S," *Electronics,* June 16, 1981.

"Managing Computer Security," *Computer Security Journal,* Winter 1982.

Martin, James, Security, Accuracy and Privacy in Computer Systems (Englewood Cliffs, N.J.: Prentice-Hall, 1973).

Marketing Consultants International, *Who, What, and Where in Communications Security,* chap. 7, (Hagerstown, Md.: MCI, Inc., June 1982).

Merkle, R.C., and M.E. Hellman, "On the Security of Multiple Encryption," *Communications of the ACM,* July 1981.

——, "Hiding Information and Receipts in Trapdoor Knapsacks," *IEEE Transactions on Information Theory IT-24,* 1978.

Morris, R., and K. Thompson, "Password Security: A Case History," *Communications of the ACM,* November 1979.

Moulton, Rolf, "A Strategy for Dealing with Computer Fraud and Abuse: A Case Study," *Computer Security Journal,* Winter 1982.

Natarajan, Thiagarajan, Ermand Centrofanti, Allen Hansel, and Philip Lioio, "Power Subsystems: Problems and Solutions," Computer Design, May 1982.

National Bureau of Standards, "Guidelines for ADP Physical Security and Risk Management," National Bureau of Standards, *FIPS PUB 31,* 1974.

——, "Computer Security Guidelines for Implementing the Privacy Act of 1974," National Bureau of Standards, *FIPS PUB 41,* 1976.

——, "Guidelines on Evaluation of Techniques for Automated Personal Identification," National Bureau of Standards, *FIPS PUB 48,* 1977.

——, "Audit and Control of Computer Security II: Systems Vulnerabilities and Controls" (Washington, D.C.: National Bureau of Standards Special Publication 500-57, 1977).

——, "An Analysis of Computer Security Safeguards for Detecting and Preventing Intentional Computer Misuse" (Washington, D.C.: National Bureau of Standards, Special Publication 500-25, 1978).

——, "Audit and Control of Computer Security" (Washington, D.C.: National Bureau of Standards Special Publication 500-19, 1978).

——, "Computer Security and the Data Encryption Standards," (Washington, D.C.: National Bureau of Standards, Special Publication 500-27, 1978).

——, "Guideline for Automatic Data Processing Risk Analysis," National Bureau of Standards, *FIPS PUB 65,* August 1979.

——, "The NBS Computer Networking Program," Institute for Computer Sciences and Technology, *NBSIR 80-2154,* August 1980.

——, *Proceedings of the Second Seminar on the DoD Computer Security Initiative Program* (Gaithersburg, Md.: National Bureau of Standards, January 15–17, 1980).

——, *Proceedings of the Fourth Seminar on the DoD Computer Security Initiative Program* (Gaithersburg, Md.: National Bureau of Standards, August 10–12, 1981).

National Fire Codes 1983 (Quincy, Mass.: National Fire Protection Association, 1983).

Nye, J.M., "Satellite Communications and Vulnerability," *Computerworld,* May 3, 1982.

O'Callaghan, P.B., A.J. Granfihler, D.K. Graham, and R.G. Bradley, "Cooperative Testing of a Positive Personnel Identifier," *Journal of the Institute of Nuclear Materials,* 1980.

Office of Management and Budget, "Circular A-71," March 6, 1965.

———, "Transmittal Memo no. 1," July 27, 1978.

Ormond, Tom, "Fiber-Optic Components," *EDN,* May 13, 1981.

Parker, Donn B., *Computer Security Management* (Reston, Va.: Reston Publishing, 1981).

———, *Crime by Computer* (New York: Scribner's, 1976).

———, "Threats to Computer Systems," *Livermore Report UCRL-13572* (Livermore Laboratories), March 1973.

"Personal Identification by Hand Geometry Parameters," *Stanford Research Institute Report,* July 15, 1969.

Peterson, W.W., and E.J. Weldon, *Error-Correcting Codes* (Cambridge, Mass.: MIT Press, 1972).

Pevovar, Ed, and Brian McGann, "Sorting through the LAN Morass," *Digital Design,* November 1982.

Pollack, Raoul, "Implications of International Terrorism on Security of Information Systems," *IEEE INFOCOM Proceedings,* April 1983.

Privacy Act of 1974, *P.L. 93-579.*

Rapoport, Roger, "The I Spies," *Western's World,* March 1983.

Reed, Susan K., and Dennis K. Branstad, "Reflections on Ten Years of Computer Security," *Computer Security,* November 1982.

Rivest, R.L., "A Description of Single-Chip Implementation of the RSA Cipher," *Lambda* (now VLSI Design), fourth quarter 1980.

———, A. Shamir, and L. Adelman, "A Method for Obtaining Digital Signatures in Public-Key Cryptosystems," *Communications of the ACM,* vol. 21, no. 2, February 1978.

Rosner, Roy D., *Distributed Telecommunications Networks* (Belmont, Ca.: Lifetime Learning Publications, 1982).

Sanders, Steve, "Voice Messaging: While You Were Out—A New System Called," *Today's Office,* October 1982.

Sardinas, Joseph L., Jr., and Richard Asebrook, "Bridging the Gap Between DP Professionals and Auditors," *Computer Security Journal,* Winter 1982.

Schweitzer, J.A. "Personal Computing and Data Security," *Security World,* June 1980.

Schmitt, Warren R., "Data Security Program Development: An Overview," *Computer Security Journal,* Winter 1982.

Schrager, Barry, "Outwitting 2-bit Thieves and Arresting Computer Crime," *Data Communications,* November 1982.

Shamir, Adi, "A Polynomial Time Algorithm for Breaking Merkle-Hellman Cryptosystems," (extended abstract for *Crypto '82*), April 1982.

———, and R.E. Zippel, "On the Security of the Merkle-Hellman Cryptographic Scheme," *IEEE Transactions on Information Theory,* May 1980.

Shaw, James K., and Stuart W. Katzke, "An Executive Guide to ADP Contingency Planning," *Computers and Security,* November 1982.

Summons, G.J., "Half a Loaf is Better Than None: Some Novel Integrity Problems," *Proceedings, 1981 Symposium on Security and Privacy,* IEEE Computer Society, April 1981.

―――, "Symmetric and Asymmetric Encryption," *Computing Surveys,* vol. 11, no. 4, December 1979.

Sloan, M.E., *Introduction to Minicomputers and Microcomputers* (Reading, Mass.: Addison-Wesley, 1980).

Spellman, Marc, "A Comparison Between Frequency Hopping and Direct Spread PN as Antijam Techniques," *IEEE Communications Magazine,* March 1983.

"Spreading Danger of Computer Crime," *Business Week,* April 20, 1981.

Swartz, Herbert, "Taking the Bite Out of Computer Crime," *Business Computer Systems,* October 1982.

Sykes, David J., "Practical Approaches to Network Security," paper presented to Computer Security and Privacy Symposium, April 29–30, 1975.

"Systems Auditability and Control Study," *Data Processing Audit Practices Report,* Institute of Internal Auditors, Altomonte Springs, Fla., 1977.

Talbot, J.P., *Management Guide to Computer Security* (New York: Wiley, 1981).

Tangney, John D., and Peter S. Tasker, "Safeguarding Today's Interactive Computer Systems," *Computer Security Journal,* Winter 1982.

"Tapping the Bank's Wires," *Newsweek,* April 25, 1983.

"Technology '83," *IEEE Spectrum,* January 1983.

Thompson, Fritz, "Death Knell for the Perfumed Love Letter," *Impact (Albuquerque Journal News Magazine),* December 1, 1981.

Trent, Darrell, Richard Morefield, and Martin Esslina, "The Deadly Game of Terrorism," *The Stanford Magazine,* Fall 1982.

Trudo, R.A., D.J. Puetz, and J.P. Sena, "Analog-Digital Testing Combined in Tech Control Center," *Data Communications,* November 1979.

Tucker, Ruxton, "The Glitch Stops Here," *Computer Design,* February 1982.

U.S. Department of Commerce, "Data Encryption Standard," *FIPS PUB 46,* January 15, 1977.

U.S. Department of Defense, "Trusted Computer System Evaluation Criteria," January 27, 1983 (final draft).

Urbanik, Theodore K. "Fiber-Optic Technology Takes to the Air," *Military Electronics / Countermeasures,* October 1982.

VanderHeyden, Eric, and Jerry Bogar, "Designing for Compliance with

FCC EMI Regulations,'' *Computer Design,* January 1982.

Van Tassel, D., *Computer Security Management* (Englewood Cliffs, N.J.: Prentice-Hall, 1972).

Wagner, C., *The CPA and Computer Fraud* (Lexington, Mass.: Lexington Books, 1979).

West, E., and others, "Standard Practice for the Fire Protection of Essential Electronic Equipment Operations" (Washington, D.C.: U.S. Dept. of Commerce RP-1, August 1978).

Whitecraft, Virginia, "The New York-San Francisco Satellite Connection," *Office Products News,* October 1981.

Wood, C.C., "Future Applications of Cryptography," *Computers and Security,* January 1982.

Zaki, Ahmed, "Regulation of Electronic Funds Transfer: Impact and Legal Issues," *Communications of the ACM,* February 1983.

Zientara, Marguerite, "Disaster Recovery: Some Like It Hot, Others Cold," *Computerworld,* September 13, 1982.

Index

About the Author

James Arlin Cooper is a supervisor of the Computer Security Division at Sandia Laboratories, Albuquerque, New Mexico. He has worked at Sandia for the past nineteen years on electromagnetic theory, radar guidance systems, electronic coded switches, unique signal generators, unique signal decoders, and computer security. He is an adjunct professor at the University of New Mexico. Dr. Cooper received the B.S. and M.S. degrees from the University of New Mexico and the Ph.D. in Electrical Engineering from Stanford University. He is also the author of *Microprocessor Background for Management Personnel.*